Roy MacGregor's

Valley Christmas

Roy MacGregor

Published by

GSPH GENERAL STORE PUBLISHING HOUSE

1 Main Street Burnstown, Ontario, Canada K0J 1G0
Telephone 1-800-465-6072 Fax (613) 432-7184

ISBN 1-896182-26-7
Printed and bound in Canada

Layout and Design by Leanne Enright
Cover Design by Tammy Anderson

General Store Publishing House gratefully acknowledges the assistance of the Ontario Arts Council and Canada Council.

Canadian Cataloguing in Publication Data

MacGregor, Roy, 1948-
Roy MacGregor's valley Christmas

ISBN 1-896182-26-7

1. Christmas stories, Canadian (English). I. Title.

PS8575.G84R69 1995 C813'.54 C95-920958-1
PR9199.1.M3174R69 1995

First Printing December 1996

Dedication

To my cousin, Don McCormick, who created—and preserves—the Christmas Classic.

Each year we grow older, it makes us younger.

Acknowledgements

The author and General Store Publishing House are grateful to *The Ottawa Citizen* and publisher Russ Mills for permission to collect these stories. For each book sold, a contribution will be made to the Ottawa Citizen Literacy Foundation, by *The Ottawa Citizen*, Roy MacGregor, and General Store Publishing House.

Table of Contents

A Christmas Curve 7

Christmas in Aerie 23

The Christmas Classic 27

Christmas on the Hill 31

The Christmas Painting 45

The Christmas Spoon 59

Shadows of Christmas Past 79

Angel with a Cowbell 83

The Magic Knife 103

The Day the Ice Turned to Glass 113

A Christmas Curve

Denzil can hear them talking again. It comes to him in snatches and reminds him of the way shore breezes once delivered talk from the island when he was still well enough to summer at the lake. It comes to him in whispers and reminds him of the way the pipes from the wood stove once carried his parents' kitchen talk upstairs when he was considered too young to know how badly things were going. It comes, fading in and out, making sense and not making sense, but like everything else that comes to Denzil M'Gorrigal these days, reminding him of other days that have long since come and gone, gone Lord knows where.

" . . . as soon after New Year's as I can get it together . . . "

" . . . they can't hold the room forever . . . "

"Yes, I'll talk to them, okay? I said I would . . . "

There is not much to be said for growing old. It is not so much the pain, but the ache. Denzil's joints have the pain, and his dresser holds pills to help; his soul gets the ache, and while his dresser drawer used to hold a bottle that helped, a bit, there is no longer even a bottle to reach for, not since the last round of tests turned up diabetes. Or was it high blood pressure? Or is that what he's going in for next week? What does it matter—at Denzil's age, no one ever passes anyway.

" . . . You can't put a lock on the outside of his door, for Heaven's sake . . . "

Denzil wanders. He wanders inside his head and outside his room, and he knows it, and he knows, too, that they are frightened by the way he sometimes wanders off. He can understand them being concerned about him getting lost physically, but why when he's just thinking? What is the harm in drifting if you go nowhere? What is it they are afraid of him running into?

And he forgets. The one truly surprising thing about growing old and forgetful is that the one thing one is constantly aware of is that you keep on forgetting things. You never forget that you can't remember, and it's embarrassing, but about the only thing you can do about it is to act like everyone else does: pretend that you didn't notice.

Denzil M'Gorrigal knows the following: he was born on the 21st of March 1914; it is today Dec. 24, 1990, but like dates on a tombstone, nothing to explain the short dash in between. And, by God, does it ever seem like a dash. Evelyn died on him seven years ago, but he can still smell her in the drawers of the dresser they let him bring along when he moved in. He still honours her place on the mattress, keeping to the left side of the bed even if it means a longer hike to the washroom at night. Make that two hikes, one at precisely 2:18 a.m., one at exactly 4:30, his bladder as dependable as the old Grand Trunk run that came up through the Madawaska Valley from Ottawa when Denzil was still a kid, and it still mattered when trains got in.

Apart from the day when he found Evelyn slumped over the peonies she was planting in the front yard—a day he could describe in exacting detail right down to the interior colours of the ambulance, right down to the words he'd used when he blew up at the doctor who'd come to tell him they'd lost her (as if they had all been married together for 44 years)—Denzil didn't retain much data from the past few decades: retired as a civil servant (Agriculture Canada), worked a bit as a commissionaire (veterans' rights), got bored silly with ham radio, wintered four times in Florida, lost Evelyn. After Evelyn, who cared if it rained or snowed, or even if the government got the boot it so richly deserved? Well, not quite—Denzil did want to live long enough to throw the scoundrels out. But as he often said, that was the only ambition left in this country.

If he went back on the other side of that dash, however, particularly if he went back and settled happily into those years toward the end of the Great Depression, particularly 1937 and 1938, the years he was courting Evelyn, then the days began to take on a different form entirely. He could remember each one with a clarity days must take on during a bus tour of Europe. Each day a new address, new menu, new language. That's how it seemed back then, back when Denzil M'Gorrigal was going to amount to something, by God, and you had better believe it.

But what had he amounted to? He never killed anyone. Never hurt anyone. Stayed married. Raised five children, some better than others. Put away enough that he didn't become a burden. Outlived his wife, and went soft in the brain. His own grandfather had gone this way. Back then they said he'd gone "off" a bit, a bit "funny." His father had it, too. They said it was "hardening of the arteries." Now Denzil has it, and he finds himself sitting in the doctor's office beside his grown daughter Mary while the doctor looks at Mary and explains to her that her father is showing signs of Alzheimer's disease. The doctor and Mary don't talk as if Denzil's not there. On the contrary, they talk about him and look at him as if he's a car she drove in, and the man at the cash is trying to convince her not to bother.

Denzil knows it is going to get worse. He knows, too, that he will not know once it does get worse, and that is as frightening a thought as those first flashes of panic that raced through his mind the afternoon he backed out the door with two iced teas in his hands and dropped both the moment he saw Evelyn. But it is not worse yet. And that is why the snippets of conversations that keep slipping out of the living room and the kitchen and the family room of his daughter's home are so discouraging.

" . . . You obviously don't understand the difference between a retirement home and a nursing home . . . "

" . . . We could turn it into a computer room maybe . . . "

Denzil does not understand this home. He has been here now for five years. He was invited in. It was their idea, not his. It made sense enough that he didn't bother putting up the fight he might have. He moved from a home where he could stare into his neighbour's windows and see what they were up to to one where the windows on the surrounding houses seemed black as sunglasses and let in nothing, certainly not curiosity. He left a backyard where growth was encouraged to come to one where growth was sprayed and hacked, a backyard of cedar deck and interlocking brick that held but one redeeming quality: when Denzil walked out to the far edge of the deck, he could see the Rideau Canal in the distance. He could watch the tour boats in summer and the skaters in winter. As long as Mary ensured he was dressed properly for it.

He moved from a small bungalow where one table was good enough for every meal to a two-storey monster with two tables, and diners who tended to eat standing up or sitting on the downstairs chesterfield. He went from a black-and-white television to colour televisions in two of the bedrooms and the kitchen, and a huge screen with lousy colour in the basement, which seemed to be tuned permanently in to the sports channel. He went from a house where he still wrote letters to one where they communicated by modem and fax machine, and had a telephone for the car. He went from a home where he and Evelyn read for relaxation to one where relaxation was thought impossible unless one held some electronic device in the hand and fired at random. Unable to keep up with the dizzying flip of the channels, Denzil hadn't watched for years. And since reading didn't stick much anymore, he spent most of his time at ease with his own remembrances, no channel selector required. The rest of the household thought him as odd as he considered them.

But that did not mean he did not love them. He adored his daughter. Mary had been the caring child of the five. Mary had been the one Denzil and Evelyn could always count on. Mary had taken him in because everyone expected her to, including Mary, including Denzil. And if he loved the Mary of his memory—a quiet little girl with brown hair and glasses, and a talent for mathematics—more than he loved the Mary of his present—a busy woman who believed "call waiting" was a gift from God—it did not mean he held anything against his grown child. She was still the best of the lot by far, even if she had married a man, Donald, who was the sort of man who answered "Donald" every time Denzil said "Don." An accountant. A man too busy spending money to wonder about what he was buying. Their children, one boy and one girl, were spoiled but terrific, which meant that Denzil could even forgive Don for being Donald so long as Denzil thought first of the kids.

Alice is 14 and pretty, and Denzil no longer wonders why a child would be given her own phone and number, complete with call waiting. Jamie is 12 and would have a terrific overbite if Mary weren't so determined to spend the price of a new car on making him look exactly like all of his friends. Of all his grandchildren—and there are now eight, or is it nine?—Denzil likes Jamie the best. They are more like brothers than grandfather and grandson. They both love sports, especially hockey. Together they laugh at the Leafs, bemoan what has become of the Canadiens, and fight happily over who is the greater threat, Gretzky or Lemieux. Donald hates hockey and plays something called "squash," which is about what you'd expect for a Donald.

On Tuesday, Denzil asked Mary if she would take him out shopping. She seemed surprised. She said she could pick up anything he needed, but Denzil insisted. He wanted to buy the kids presents with his own money, picked out by his own hand—though he ended up needing a bit of help when it came to Alice. Mary's first suggestion, an answering machine, was too pricey. Her second, the new Phil Collins' CD, was perfect, though Denzil hadn't a clue who Phil Collins was or what the initials CD stood for—no matter, Mary seemed satisfied, and Mary, of course, always knew what was best.

"Just leave me here for a bit," he told Mary when they passed in front of the mall's main department store.

Mary seemed startled. "I'll help," she said, as if there would be no further discussion of the matter.

"You just sit down over there," Denzil said with a firmness that surprised him. "In 15 minutes you can come get me if I'm not back."

"Why?"

"I want it to be a secret."

Mary looked at her father, the same questioning look Denzil had seen in other circumstances, when Jamie might ask if he could walk off to the corner store alone, the look far more questioning of herself and her own value as a proper parent than of the boy and his intentions. Denzil smiled at his daughter. "I'm not a child, Mary. You don't have to worry."

Mary could only nod. Which was all Denzil needed.

The first young man Denzil bumped into, who wasn't wearing a winter coat, he asked where he might find the sports department. He followed a pointing finger and, eventually, came around a 60-foot ski rack to find what he had come for: hockey sticks. He picked one out. It seemed warped. He picked out another. It was warped even worse. He crossed the aisle and took off another. It was warped the wrong way.

Denzil carried the stick until he came to another young man who wasn't wearing a winter coat. The man was stacking ski wax, and Denzil had to clear his throat six times before the young man asked the obvious.

"Can I help you?"

"All your hockey sticks are warped."

"Curved. Right curve. Left curve. Illegal curves are marked."

"I just want a plain, simple hockey stick."

The young man stood up, looking curiously at Denzil. "That's what you've got in your hand, sir."

"I don't want the warp."

The young man took the stick, looking at it. "This is a right. You want a left."

"A hockey stick. I want a plain stick."

"They come in right and left."

"A plain stick."

"You want straight?"

Denzil nodded, finally getting through to the young man. The young man shook his head. "No such thing. Sorry."

"What do you mean, 'no such thing'?"

"No one makes straight."

"No one?"

"No."

Denzil walked back with his stick and put it back. He checked up and down the aisles. A thousand sticks, a thousand curves. He found some less warped than others, but then couldn't decide whether he should buy left or right. He figured Jamie must be the same as him—they both loved the game, after all—and determined Jamie must, therefore, shoot left, and he took the one with an "L" on the handle and, from what he could determine, the least warp possible. But it still looked more like a scythe than a hockey stick to Denzil M'Gorrigal. He picked up a puck as well, walked up to the counter, paid cash and walked out just as Mary was coming in.

"You did it!" she said, a little too excited, a bit too much smiling.

Denzil said nothing. The last time he'd heard that phrase and seen that smile on his overly-organized daughter it was directed at Jamie, who'd just figured out what to do with his pottie.

~~~
~~~

It is two o'clock in the morning. Christmas Day. Denzil lies on the left side of the bed and cannot sleep. He heard Mary come in a half-hour ago, Mary off to midnight mass on her own, Donald claiming he was too tired to join her. Too drunk might be more to the point. Donald opening what he called an $80 bottle of cognac to celebrate Christmas Eve and drinking, by Denzil's estimate, $62.34 worth before he sagged, with the channel selector on his lap, and began snoring. The kids were out with their friends caroling. At least that's what they had told Mary, and that's certainly what Mary had wanted to hear. Denzil looked out his upstairs window sometime after 11, though, and could have sworn he saw Jamie and one of his chums slide by on the back bumper of a car that had just come through the four-way stop.

Denzil was glad to go to bed, even if he couldn't sleep. He'd wrapped the thing called the CD and then the hockey stick and puck—the stick in a billowing bag that, with luck, would disguise the blade—and carried them in from the living room himself to put them under the tree. Donald, at about the $16-level of his bottle, had been in less than full spirit.

"Pretty hard to hide a hockey stick," he'd said.

"I guess," Denzil had replied. He didn't care.

"Jamie likes to pick out his own, you know."

Denzil said nothing.

"That right or left?" Donald wanted to know.

Denzil couldn't remember.

"Better not be a right," Donald said. "Jamie shoots left. Like me."

Denzil couldn't resist. "When did you ever play?"

Donald smiled. "There's a lot you don't know about me."

Denzil kept his mouth shut. Not nearly as much as you don't know about me, Donny.

But now he couldn't sleep for worrying that Donald was right. What if he had bought the wrong stick? What if Jamie didn't like it? Denzil lay in his bed and squirmed. He wished Evelyn was there. She'd know what to do. He wished his brain worked better. Once he would have known what to do himself.

Denzil knew he should be able to think this out. He had seen Jamie play a hundred times or more, hadn't he, and how did Jamie hold his stick? He tried to think back but Jamie was like a ghost bouncing through his brain, half-focussed, drifting in and out, gone. He thought he saw him once bursting in across the blue-line, but then the ghost took focus, and it was Tommy Deschenes breaking out over the Bonnechere River with that hard rap rap of the stick that Tommy used to do when he wanted the puck.

Denzil sat up. What was that rapping? Somebody at the door? No. It was 2:15, almost time to go to the bathroom. He went, moving carefully, listening for the rapping, but all he could hear was the sound of Donald snoring and the heavy deep-sleep breathing coming from Jamie's room. Jamie's Gretzky poster was on the door, facing out, and in the half-light of the night-lite Mary kept in the hall for Denzil's bladder runs, he tried to make out Gretzky enough to see which way the star shot, and see if he could then remember which way Jamie shot. Then maybe he'd remember which one he'd bought. Gretzky was a left shot, at least in the picture. Denzil took his own old stance from the Bonnechere River. Same as Gretzky's. Surely to God the same as Jamie's. Denzil raced to the bathroom, like today's trains—overdue.

~~~

Now he was out on the ice. What a crazy thing to do. He must have gotten dressed—obviously he'd gotten dressed—and now here he was in the middle of the night, Christmas morning, stepping down the stairs leading to the canal, the black ice shining, like church shoes, in the distant street lights. In his right hand he has Jamie's Christmas present, the new stick. In his left hand he holds the puck. His feet are in the big rubber-soled snow boots that Mary had forced on him last winter after he slipped and fell on his elbow. No skates.

Now this, Denzil tells himself with a smile, is wandering. He is out here alone. Christmas morning and there are no work crews flooding. Christmas morning and there are no skaters. Just one old man, a hockey stick that might be wrong, a puck, and fat flakes beginning to fall so slowly they drift through the street lights as if passing through shining water.

How did he get out without being noticed? Denzil does not know and, frankly, does not care. He knows he did a good job of dressing. He is warm, sweating even. And the stick and puck have obviously been unwrapped without Mary hearing the sound of the paper and tape. Strange, for on other nights Mary can hear him hit the toilet seat at 2:18, and again at 4:30, if he doesn't take special care.
~~~

He cannot properly grip the stick unless he drops the puck, so he does, and it slaps on the ice like a voice from the past. He takes the stick and sets it down. It feels wrong but he knows it is right. Right as in correct, for it is left, and Denzil was a left shot when he played on the Bonnechere for the Black Donald Gang. But it feels terribly wrong all the same, like a lacrosse stick lacking the catgut. He tries to work the puck with it, but the forehand feels more like pulling than pushing, and the backhand sends the puck drifting off ahead of him. It is impossible to stickhandle.

Careful on his boots, Denzil moves forward to get the puck.

RAP RAP.

He turns, a shadow flicking to the side of him. Nothing. He pushes with his back foot, sliding toward the puck, reaching with his ridiculous stick.

RAP RAP.

He stops, turns again. By the street light, large flakes glistening in dark, curly hair, is Tommy Deschenes. He is wearing one of the old Black Donald wool sweaters. His lower legs bulge with catalogues. He has on a pair of skates that lace up and strap over, straight blade, no tube. He is rapping a perfectly straight, one-piece, solid-elm stick on the ice.

"C'mon Denny, send 'er over."

RAP RAP.

Denzil does not know what to do. He cannot speak. Instinctively, because now Tommy is more clear than anything he has seen since the day Evelyn died, he reaches for the puck and pushes it, slightly off because of the curve, and the air suddenly fills with the glorious rasp of Tommy Deschenes' skates as he moves into the pass, his stick rapping the ice as he knocks the puck from side to side and then, swift and graceful as a caged cat, turns back on Denzil.

The air is sharp in Denzil's nose, quick in his lungs. He has not breathed so deeply, so fast in years. It tastes wonderful. He moves to the side as Tommy comes back up ice, and finds that he has shot to the side, his feet gliding in a manner that bumps a corner of his memory that has been sleeping far too long. He does not have to look down to know he has his skates on. He does not have to ask to know that he should try to check Tommy.

He stares down the ice at Tommy. Tommy is laughing. His eyes sparkle like the snow Denzil was watching fall through the cone of the street lights. Tommy Deschenes, killed at Normandy, laughing as he bears down on Denzil M'Gorrigal.

Denzil pokes, misses, and moves opposite to Tommy's shoulder fake, and it works as Tommy comes straight back, expecting otherwise. Denzil has him, but suddenly Denzil has lost him. Tommy drops the puck back from his straight stick and it strikes first one blade of his skates and then the other and then darts past Denzil into the open ice, a double-bank of the puck that Tommy has executed without so much as breaking stride, a play that has worked for him a thousand times and has never, ever been mastered by another member of the Black Donald Gang.

Tommy turns, pops the puck up into Denzil's glove and stops, the ice sheering and flying in a high, gentle curve over Denzil's pants, where it sticks.

"The rest of the gang's waiting," Tommy says.

No explanation. Nothing. Just the rest of the gang is waiting, and Denzil knows exactly what Tommy means. Together they head off down the canal, two dark figures passing a puck back and forth, the one rapping loudly each time he wants a pass and laughing when he gets it, only now it is not the canal, it is the Bonnechere itself, and Denzil knows exactly where he is and where they will be. In out of the wind, beyond the point. He can see the sparks of the camp-fire floating high through the thick flakes.

Denzil still hasn't spoken. He drops his stick in with the others, pockets his puck and sits on the balsam boughs to take off his skates. His toes are cold and he takes off his woollen sock and rubs his toes with snow, wincing as the old feeling comes back into them. If only it was as easy for his head.

"I brought you some tea."

He looks up and there is a young woman standing in front of him. She has a large toque on and several scarfs, but he does not need to see anything more than the huge eyes and the small smile. Evelyn. She hands him the metal cup, he sips, and with his sock back on and boot unlaced, he hops over to the fire beside her, and they are all there. Lucy Dombrowski who died of cancer. Lonnie Manchura who went West, and nobody ever heard of again. Teen Wilkinson who went off to medical school and came back home to practise. Polly who never married. Bill who married three times. Wally who turned into a drunk. Joe who made a fortune selling cottages. Marie who became reeve herself after her husband died.

Only now, no one is dead. They are sitting around a magnificent fire of pine boughs and cedar and dried birch, and there is tea in the pot, and they are all singing along with Teen Wilkinson who has cut the fingers out of a pair of gloves so he can play the accordion. And Denzil, who cannot remember to lift the toilet seat, finds he not only remembers all the words, but is leading the singsong: "I Got Plenty 'o Nuthin'", "Blue Moon", "Pennies from Heaven", "Smoke Gets in Your Eyes", "Stardust" . . .

How did he get here? He cannot remember. It does not matter. He is here and that is all that matters. He can feel the snow melt on his burning cheeks, catches one of the big flakes in his eyelash as he looks up into the night for the best effect to end "Smoke Gets in Your Eyes". He wonders if Phil—what?—Collins ever heard of Hoagy Carmichael, wonders if Alice will ever sit around a fire and sing songs with her friends. He can taste the tea, the rim of the cup so cool, the lap of the liquid against his lips so deliciously warm. He can hear the fire snapping. He can hear Teen Wilkinson's fingers keeping warm with silly ditties while Teen waits for the next song to be called out. He can see and talk to and touch all the friends who ever truly mattered to him.

Yes, touch. He can touch Evelyn's cheek when they walk off from the fire and around to the far side of the point. He can touch her lips, her eyes. He can touch his lips to hers. And he can smell her when she hugs back and he leans down to snuggle his face in between her scarf and warm neck. The smell reminds him of his dresser drawer, which makes him laugh, thinking how impossible it would be to explain.

Gradually the night wears on, and the gang wears down. A few peel away and head off to skate home down along the Bonnechere to the first dam where there's a trail leading up to the Dombrowski farm and beyond. Teen Wilkinson's old man comes along in his cutter, and when he stops, the steam rises from the horses faster than from the boiling tea. The team snorts and paws at the ice, ice shoes catching, eager to be off again, and the kids pile in among the buffalo blankets and Hudson's Bay blankets and tossed hay, and off they go into the night, bells jingling and skis sighing and horses snorting and kids still singing.

"I have to go."

Denzil turns and it is Evelyn. She has on her skates. Tommy Deschenes is waiting off to the side, fiddling with a couple of hockey sticks and laughing. Tommy is Evelyn's neighbour. If they skate in the other direction they can be home in half the time they'd take if old man Wilkinson dropped them off in the cutter. Tommy is lighting a smoke, and it strikes Denzil that he never sees anyone smoke like that anymore. Tommy kisses the cigarette, sucks hard once the cup of his hand comes down, he shakes off the match and draws deep, letting some of the smoke fall out of his mouth and up and in through his nostrils. Denzil had forgotten how important it once was to smoke gracefully. Now, when he sees people light up, they look like they're sneaking the vestry wine.

He knows better than to kiss Evelyn in front of Tommy. Out of sight, fine, but never in public like this. He can only smile at her, wishing he could grab her and tell her what's coming, but he knows he cannot. She can't know about the children. He can't possibly tell her about the peonies. He mustn't mention Normandy, even though Tommy wouldn't, right now, have the foggiest notion where it is. He smiles back exactly the way he would have on a cold winter's night in 1937: his mouth not quite working properly, his grin a bit off, his overbite a bit gawky.

"See you, then," he says. Evelyn smiles shyly and turns towards Tommy.

"Where'd ya get this danged stick?" Tommy asks.

"A Christmas present," Denzil says without thinking.

"Santa must be having a yuk on you, pal," Tommy says, laughing himself. "She's bent so bad you can't even use her."

"Supposed to be like that," Denzil says.

Tommy raps it twice and pulls the puck. It shoots off when he puts it on his backhand. "Cripes!" he says, and chases after the runaway puck, kicking it back through his skates in the manner only Tommy Deschenes could master. He slaps it back toward Denzil. "You got took, lad," he says, laughing.

Evelyn has the teapot and it rattles with the cups. The beauty of winter is you can let the fire die down on its own. If only life could be so kind. She passes by Denzil and touches her mitten to his arm as she moves past, and the touch is as flushing warm and ticklish as—oh my God—the feeling Denzil had last month when they pumped him full of barium for the X-rays. He wants to stop her, explain, but he cannot speak, and the only sound is the rasp of Evelyn's skates as she hurries to catch Tommy Deschenes, who is rapping a puck from side to side as he scoots from one open windsweep of ice to the next.

Denzil stands alone on the ice of the Rideau Canal, a taxi passing by on the Queen Elizabeth Way, the tires sizzling on the salt and snow and pavement. There is nothing he can do but pick up his stick and puck, and head back home to Mary's, careful not to slip on the steps. The snow is heavier now, and the walking is much easier. The slippage now is all in his head.

"Where the hell did you get this thing, anyway?"

The voice belongs to Donald. The answer is supposed to be his, Denzil knows, but cannot follow. Donald is standing in the kitchen holding up Jamie's hockey stick while Denzil loads up his coffee with sugar. The kids and Mary are still by the tree, too far away to hear, too engrossed in the presents to care.

"It's okay. I checked," Denzil says. "He shoots the same way I used to, you know. Left."

"Look at it, for Christ's sake."

Denzil looks and sees a hockey stick. He does not remember taping it, which is fine: he doesn't remember a lot of things.

"It's perfectly straight!" Donald says.

Denzil looks again. It is straight. But he tried it. It worked. Same as Gretzky shoots. Same as he once shot. Same for Jamie. What's the fuss?

But Donald isn't through. "Where'd you get this thing. It must have been in their stock room for half a century or more." He's laughing. Not laughing with, but at—at Denzil.

"Mary took me up to the mall. I bought it."

"Jesus Murphy, old man—you won't catch a kid using something like this. You should'a let me pick one up for you. He won't want to use this."

Mary is at the door now, listening. Denzil can sense her presence, sense her calling Donald off with hand signals and facial expressions. He sees Donald's furrowed brow, his mouth turn in disgust, his jaw tense as he shuts it on command.

"Donald," Mary says in that voice she has used since childhood when she is about to lie, "can you get me something up from the basement." It means she wants to talk to her husband. Denzil could care less. He didn't sleep well last night. He's tired, and tired of Donald. He has his coffee and the only present he's looked forward to since Evelyn left: a box of English toffee. He's just going to sit here and sip and suck like a very old man, and anybody who doesn't like it can . . .

"Grandpa?"

Denzil turns. It is Jamie, smiling through his braces, the stick in his hand held out.

"This is really neat," the boy says. "Where'd you get it?"

Denzil would like to speak but cannot. The right side of his teeth are caught in the toffee. He can only smile, as if it's some great secret where he got it.

"I'm going to put it on my wall," Jamie says. "Right up there with Gretzky."

Finally, Denzil breaks free his teeth. "I bought it to be used," he says, a bit more brusquely than intended. His emotions—stuck on Donald—haven't caught up to his words, intended for Jamie.

Jamie smiles sheepishly. "Yah, well. Maybe I could try it sometime. But I'd be careful."

The doorbell rings and the boy is gone. Christmas winding down. Soon the wrapping will be put in the green garbage bag. Soon the calls will be made to the aunts and uncles, and Denzil will be put on to prove he's still alive. Everyone will ask if he got his toffee. He won't have the nerve to say five boxes, five children, five boxes. Soon the presents will be forgotten. Soon the stores will open, and Mary and Alice will head out to buy what they really need. Soon Denzil will be taken for a drive to see an absolutely remarkable place that he just has to say the word if he doesn't like . . .

Mary and Donald want to take him for a walk. Denzil's stomach has been flaring up. Too much toffee. He thinks it is the Feast of St. Stephan's but only because Mary and Alice are not out shopping, which must mean there are no stores open. He's not sure. He only knows that never before have both Mary and Donald asked him along for a walk, so it must be important. They haven't the nerve to tell him indoors.

"We thought you'd enjoy seeing the skaters," Mary says.

They walk down along the canal, the ice now covered in more fabric and colour than Denzil could ever have imagined possible back when they all wore the same colour and the same material on the Bonnechere. Mary and Donald discuss the obvious: the colours, the people, the sunlight. It is even more obvious that they are merely gathering themselves for the inevitable.

It is so bright that it makes Denzil wince. He cannot see when he looks to the south. The snow is too white, too bright. The sun, too strong. All he can do is listen, listen to the shrieks and the laughter and the disgusting piped-in music and the tires sizzling in the background.

Rap rap.

Whhhattt? Denzil looks but cannot see. He hears Tommy. He needs to see Evelyn. He has something to tell her, but he cannot remember what.

RAP RAP.

"It's Jamie, Dad—can't you see him?"

The voice belongs to Mary. But no, he cannot see. He shields his eyes and looks where she points. It is indeed Jamie. He has on a ski jacket in colours Denzil cannot even pronounce. He is wearing the $275-skates Donald bought him for Christmas. But he has the old stick, and he is rapping it on the ice, waiting for a pass from one of his friends. And when he gets the pass he races over, stickhandling back and forth. Rap rap rap.

Jamie stops in front of them, looking up onto the sidewalk where they are walking.

"I told you I'd try it."

Denzil stares down, surprised. "Is it okay?"

Jamie laughs. "I can't hang onto the puck. I keep losing it."

"Show them," the friend says.

"Show us what?" Donald asks.

"You should see Jamie's new move," the friend says.

"Watch!" Jamie shouts, and breaks away, turning along the far side of the canal like a cat—wait!—like Tommy Deschenes, down low and so smooth and quick the pace doesn't break, and he comes back toward his friend rapping the puck awkwardly against the old stick until, as he comes on to his friend, the puck falls off the stick and back into his feet. Off one blade, off the other, kicked past the friend and Jamie is away and free, circling like a cat—Tommy!—once again and coming back to stop with an exaggerated spray.

"Who taught you that?" Mary asks.

"No one," Jamie says. "It happened by accident. This stick's no good for carrying the puck—sorry, Grandpa—and when I kept losing it I kept trying to kick it back up with one skate. But if I let it bounce off both skates it happens all by itself."

"You can't stop him," says the friend.

"Show me again," Denzil says.

"Sure," the kids shout, and break away for the other side of the canal.

"We'll just be on up ahead, Dad," Mary says. "We'll wait for you."

And Denzil M'Gorrigal is left alone to watch and listen. He stands, grinning happily, as he watches his grandson move in across the Bonnechere River, the old stick rapping on the ice, Denzil and Evelyn straining through their mittens to touch every cell of each other's bodies, both of them laughing at crazy Tommy as he shows his trick with the puck again and again, no one able to understand why it keeps on working, and why no one will ever stop him, until that day, more than seven years from now, when he runs screaming up a beach he's never even heard of, Evelyn fading in and fading out, the day making sense and not making sense, Jamie stabbing the finest Christmas present of Denzil M'Gorrigal's long life high into the air like he'd just done the most astonishing thing in the history of the game, the smell of Evelyn, the sound of a bus stopping, the feel of her hand through the mitten, slipping . . .

And with the wind just right, Denzil hears parts of what Mary and Donald are saying as they move on up the sidewalk.

"I said I would tell him and I will . . . "

"Once he agrees to just go there and see, he'll be sold, you watch . . . "

"I know we can't have another night like the last, okay. We're all agreed on that . . . "

Christmas in Aerie

At first, coming to Christmas dinner was just a short walk across the top of the hill, barely time for a nostril to lock. But later, once the second generation had moved out of the Valley to bring the third closer to schools and a few added opportunities they would come to regret, Christmas dinner began with an endless drive through Algonquin Park, the roads bare of other traffic and even sand, the only music—for the family was tone-deaf, and the radio out of all range—the sound of the tire chains dirging up Smoke Lake hill and singing past the Opeongo turn.

It was the sounds that stayed with you. Not the first sight of smoke rising from the old people's winter home on the edge of the hill, not the first lick of heat that met you at the door, not the smell of turkey, the promises below the tree, not even the steam rising off the backs of the surly hogs in the pen at the foot of the hill.

No, it was what you heard: the chains that sang out each new arrival, the muffled pop of fast-moving doors, the rifle report of the party crackers, the laughter, the screaming that hurtled down off the toboggan hill and rose again as cheers from the cleared rink on the edge of the lake.

But above all, it was the voice of Santa Claus. He stood by—well, actually, was suspended from—a wall in the kitchen, the blush long since faded from his cheeks, and his tongue hanging down to the height of a five-year-old from the floor.

It was in this tongue—a narrow, flexible, red, vinyl cord, unevenly serrated on the back—that the magic of Christmas resided, for every few minutes the old woman in charge of the dinner would back away from the wood stove, wipe her hands on her apron, push through the crowd of grandchildren gathered near the tip of the hanging tongue, and she would make Santa talk.

Her thumbnail pressed tight to the serrated back of the cord, and her fingers wrapped loosely around the rest, the old woman would whip down the entire length of Santa's remarkable tongue and, for a moment, the kitchen would be filled with his message: "Mer-ry Churisssmus, evvvery-bodddy."

Sometimes she would do it too fast and Santa would squeak slightly, sometimes too slow and he would growl, but the old woman with the hard thumbnail was the one who could best make him understood.

When the grandchildren tried, what would come out of Santa's mouth was the half whistle a small hand makes when it rubs too quickly along something smooth. Santa at these times sounded more like the wind that was forming lassoes of loose snow down toward the well.

But she could make him talk, and for her Christmas Day was a race between the demands of the wood stove and the calls of the small. It was, as anyone will tell you, another time, a time when there was simply no question about who belonged where on a Christmas Day.

The women belonged in the kitchen and around the large table where the meal would eventually be eaten. The children belonged outside on the ice or inside at the tip of Santa's tongue. And the men... well, it was another time, wasn't it?

The old man—a Park ranger who'd simply refused to retire—would have sawn enough slabs, and split enough kindling, to heat the entire Upper Ottawa Valley, but there could never be enough.

While he, who prided himself on never having a drop of the demon in his house, sat in his rocker and teased any child who happened to be eyeing the skirt of the tree, the younger men took to the woodshed, where the gnaw of a Swede saw would soon eat into the laughter that followed each lie about the the size of a certain lake trout or the number of partridge in a given shot line.

No one in the kitchen ever asked for wood, and when the men would file back in with thin loads and thick tongues, no one would bother pointing out that the bin was already filled, and the turkey all but done. The call of the woodshed was simply part of the Christmas tradition.

In later years, long after the old ranger and his wife were gone, and the house on the hill was no more, long after slab wood was a word no longer used, and central heating had come to all, such gatherings would be marked by a crisis in the basement, a broken pump or a stubborn problem in the plumbing, that would insist that the men of a certain age head down until the crisis had passed, and the faces returned as flushed as they ever had from the woodshed.

In later years still, the problems would be with their own plumbing, but back then, Christmas was, in part at least, a celebration of what can go conveniently wrong.

There was, back in the days when the ranger's house still stood on the hill, a certain five-year-old who had cried louder than the tire chains coming down off Smoke Lake hill, the victim of a shocking oversight, as Santa had taken the cookies but neglected to leave behind the ordered drum.

It was a gloom that not even the old woman's hard nail on the back on Santa's tongue could lift. How dare he say, "Merrry Chrissss-mus, evreebuddeeee," when he himself had contrived to make it the most miserable gathering in history?

Too young for the woodshed, the boy could only mope around the box stove and wait for the sparks and the roar when the old ranger felt it time to improve the draw. The old man even let the youngster stoke at one point, but not even the chance to light a match under strict supervision could lift the disappointment over the missing drum.

Nor was the dinner much comfort, though the steam rose from the potatoes, a drumstick was offered, and the old ranger made a great show of unfolding the crêpe hat from his party cracker and pulling it down over his eyes.

When it was over, and the boy was sitting on the narrow steps leading up into the roughed-in sleeping room, the old ranger came to the foot of the stairs with a package that had not been under the tree. It had no bow, no name, nothing but the scraps of wrapping paper barely hiding something that was certainly round and obviously tin. He motioned the sulking boy upstairs ahead of him.

With the old ranger sitting on the edge of his bed, in what was far more loft than second floor, the boy ripped open the paper, but could not release the two wooden sticks that were heavily taped to the side of the cylinder. The old man brought out his jackknife, cut one free and let the boy join in cutting free the second.

"Stay up here," he said. "You won't be bothering anyone that way."

Later he brought up a coal-oil lamp and stayed long enough for an entire parade of drummers to pass, but then went back down at the sound of teacups, while the boy stayed behind to march again and again and again....

Eventually he tired enough to put down the sticks, and he lay in the bed with an arm around the drum, an eye on the shadows dancing against the far wall, and an ear to the pipes, listening while the delicious Valley mix of Irish and Scotch and German and Polish and French came riding up with the heat, and told him that it was at least as warm down there as it was up here where the heat was rising.

And every once in a while, rising up through the far grating near the kitchen, there would come the quick march of sensible heels on linoleum, the cheers of whatever kids were still waiting, and the whisk of a hard thumbnail on serrated vinyl. And over the laughter, and the growl of burning slab wood in twisting pipes, a remarkable voice would speak for the house that no longer stands on the edge of the hill.

"Merrrrr-eeee Chrisssmussss, evvereeebuddddeeeeee..."

The Christmas Classic

Ever since the first snow came and decided to stay, I have been thinking about the Christmas Classic.

You wouldn't know about it—at least not by that name—and you wouldn't care who wins or loses the Christmas Classic any more than those who will be playing. But that doesn't mean it isn't important to us all.

The Christmas Classic is but one small and deeply personal example of a lot of goofy traditions that most of us will be keeping this week.

They are odd commodities, these family traditions, in that their true value can be known only when they end, and it is a fear of them coming to a close, as much as anything else, that causes us all to hang on so desperately to curious habits.

Take the Christmas Classic.

It is really nothing but a game of road hockey played at the end of a gravel road, near the river.

But it is also a dance that goes on every year: the same music, the same steps, the same hall. Only the dancers change. First, to their own regret; one day, to everyone's.

Christmas begins with the drive through the Park. First it was to a small, hopelessly crowded house in a village of five houses. Now it is to a growing town and a house grown far too large for its permanent occupants.

But no matter: Christmas evens things out. No matter how large the house, there is never enough room.

Sometime during the drive the radio will fade out, and voices that should be left on barren landscapes will take over.

Someone will point out the turn where we once went in to pick up the old lumberman, and it will be remembered again, as it is every year at this time, how once the car began spinning on an icy hill and how, with the old lumberman shaking his head in disgust, the car came to rest on a ledge leaning out over the frozen lake.

Thanks to time, it has become funny.

In the small town, the meal will already be prepared. A friend from kindergarten will show at the front door at the precise minute the first line forms for plates. Someone will remark on his timing, just as they have been doing for 36 years since that kindergarten class let out for the summer.

And again, it will be as funny as it was last time he knocked.

There will be wine. A generation ago it was straight, burning drinks out in the woodshed. Then, for a while after customs changed, there was more drink inside than was ever necessary. Customs keep changing, and the way things are going, the next generation may well end up back in the woodshed.

But so much of what happens never changes. The children who now have grown children still wake up Christmas morning to find stockings laid out from Santa. The same new pair of socks. The same small box of raisins.

There is always something to mark the day. A new baby. A missing face. Last year, someone walked in on the 82-year-old giving in to the six-year-old for a quick puff on a roll-your-own, and of course, this year, it will seem funny.

That is not to say all is laughter. But on this one day, this imperfect and vastly extended family is able to come together as no other day will permit.

And nothing so demonstrates that as the Christmas Classic.

First there will be the shovelling. Those who shovelled their first shinny rink in the 1940s will join shovels with those who cannot imagine a time before snowblowers, and they will work together to build an arena that now holds more memories than the Montreal Forum.

The gaps are astonishing: age as much as ability. Some who dreamed of making the game their life facing off with some that never in their life had even been to a game. But none of this matters.

All that really matters is that one middle-aged man will, at one point in the game, blind-side a younger brother.

Someone will complain that a goal was scored by an illegal golf shot.

Someone will take a shot where it hurts.

And though not a soul will witness the Christmas Classic, the arguments will go on long into the night over which side won and which side cheated.

Arguments that, a year from now, will pick up precisely where they left off.

Christmas on the Hill

No one knows why it does so—possibly because no one has ever been around before to see—but on Christmas Eve the snow falls differently on Parliament Hill than at any other time of winter.

High above the Library, in the glow that spreads from the display lights, the big flakes fall like feathers in a vacuum, which the cynics would surely say is appropriate. Between the West Block and the Centre Block, where Queen Victoria stands as stone-faced in death as she ever was alive, the light wind from the river plays on the buildings so that the snow falls like silver coins through water, which the critics would also love. And out by the Peace Tower, where the red and blue and white and purple and green lights are strung and have been on for weeks, the snow falls and melts instantly in the small circles of shining, coloured heat, the softest hiss the Hill has heard in what has been a very long year.

At the back of the Centre Block one single yellow light spreads from a third-floor window. Anyone who happened to be passing by in a sleigh could look in and catch a solitary man sitting at a desk, staring at his hands. He is Mr. T.D.M. Sawchuk, the Honourable Member for Qu'Appelle-Gumbo in the western province of Saskatchewan. He is looking for calluses.

T.D.M. Sawchuk—his friends call him Tommy, his mother, in certain moods, would call him Thomas D'Arcy McGee as if each name was delivered by the back of the hand instead of the tongue—has been sitting at this desk for three hours and only recently noticed his hands. His Christmas Eve meal is in front of him: half a cafeteria sandwich he found in the little office refrigerator he shares with the Honourable Member for Manitou Lake, a diet Sprite he drinks when he is being political, a bottle of brandy he sips on when he is not, and a Jos. Louis cake he got from the candy machine on the basement floor. Merry Christmas, Tommy.

He has stacked the Christmas cards he has received this year around the surface of his huge desk. He has separated them into two groupings, one signed by machine, one by human hand. The machines outnumber the people by more than 100. The people, he notices, have sent him cards featuring winter scenes and religious verse; the machines have sent him words certain to offend no one and beautiful colour photographs of families, only one member of which he ever recognizes. The photographs show endless happy families and, more often than not, a happy dog. Knowing the one member of each family portrait—the man, invariably, and a fellow Honourable Member—Tommy also knows a fair bit of the truth behind these photographs. He wonders where the women find their smiles. He wonders if there is a room somewhere in the basement of the Centre Block where they supply subsidized dogs for the annual portrait.

The real Christmas cards number fewer than two dozen. With all but one exception they come from home, which is a word Tommy Sawchuk loves to use, but no longer has. Some are scenes of Saskatchewan, one of the Qu'Appelle Valley, and for a moment, T.D.M. Sawchuk can feel the way his blood always rises into his face the moment the car falls off Highway 6 heading north, falls off the flat plain and dips so quickly down into the valley that for a brief shocking moment the incredible beauty of his country seems to pull over him like a warm comforter.

It is the moment when Tommy always feels he is home. Always felt he was home. In a drawer of this same desk is a letter from a lawyer, and Tommy has no need to read it more than once. Alice is seeking a divorce, and though he knows some of his colleagues, say the Honourable Member for Lost Mountain, would be vowing revenge for such a letter, the soft hands of the Honourable Member for Qu'Appelle-Gumbo did not even tremble when they signed the postie's clipboard for registered mail. For three years, he has been expecting such a document, and for most of those three years, he has been hoping it would arrive, though now it is here he does not feel as he thought he might. Information can burn in the gut as well as brandy but it is not at all the same sensation.

Tommy knows more about Alice than what is in the letter. He knows, thanks to a contact system built up over 20 years as campaign worker, constituency executive, constituency president, candidate and, finally, sitting member for Qu'Appelle-Gumbo, that Alice has left home to spend the winter with their daughter, Jennifer, in Victoria, where Jennifer is about to graduate. He knows, thanks to a young special assistant who made friends with Jennifer the summer she was on the staff of the Honourable Member for Batoche, that Jennifer planned to take her mother to Hawaii for the holidays, and so when he thinks about them, he does not see home, where the snow moves in angry lassoes over the fields, and where you turn into the farm drive with a prayer that somewhere below there is gravel. He sees them somewhere on a beach, reading thick paperbacks that require just enough concentration that there is no room in their thoughts for him. Why should it be otherwise?

No, when the Honourable T.D.M. Sawchuk thinks of Christmas at home, he does not see Alice or Jennifer but his own parents who are now both dead and buried in the little cemetery on the back way into town. Dominic Sawchuk and Kate McGee Sawchuk: the Ukrainian and Irish blood that combines so unpredictably in Tommy. His father had been a quiet man, his mother an outgoing woman, and together they had lived through enough of the 20th century to see their prospects move from a sod house, where Dominic Sawchuk was born, to the House of Commons, where their first-born was sent.

Every Christmas for as long as Tommy Sawchuk could remember, his father had gone to the local bank, traded a dollar bill for a silver dollar and, on Christmas Day just before mass, walked out across the snow-swept fields to where the sod hut had stood. Here, in the bitter wind, Dominic Sawchuk would say a silent prayer of thanks and drop the silver dollar into the shallow depression, that still remained, where his own father and mother had scooped out the muck for the walls.

It was his wishing well, his penitence box, his small, symbolic repayment for all he believed the land had given him. And for the 10 years that Kate McGee Sawchuk survived her husband, she had kept up the Christmas Day ritual, stopping in at the bank and walking, alone, out to where the hut once stood and her husband once remembered so that she, too, could remember and be thankful. Tommy wondered if her silver dollars would still be there if he dug for them. His father had always presumed that the coins worked their way into the ground the way stones worked their way out in the field, and he put their spring disappearance down to soft soil and clay and the unholy tangle of cudweed and Indian tobacco that lay dead and grey in the sucking depression when the snow finally cleared.

The Honourable T.D.M. Sawchuk wished he could be so happily naive as his father had been. The silver dollars had ended up in his own pocket after a bit of sloppy rubber-boot walking out to the depression and, sometimes a little, sometimes a lot of rooting around in the tangle. They were cashed at the next town down the line so the local bank would not make the obvious connection, and the four quarters Tommy received each spring for his father's Christmas wish would take him well into summer with Saturday-afternoon chocolate bars. All of which, incidentally, tasted far superior to a Jos. Louis on Christmas Eve.

Looking back, that spring ritual now stands out as the first political act of the Honourable T.D.M. Sawchuk's career. The art of moving money around. The willingness to deceive. The talent for secrecy. The care he took for his own ambitious stomach.

It is in staring at his hands that Tommy realizes how much he now envies his father, whose own hands always looked as if they had just bubbled up out of the ground like the stones they were forever lifting and getting scraped on. His father was a true believer. He believed if you worked hard, it would pay off. He believed if you prayed hard, it would be answered. He believed if you were good, good things would happen back. He died in the field, found by Kate, with his heart burst and a rock beside him that only a darn fool would try and lift. Kate believed, and Tommy tended to agree, that he had died doing exactly what he would have wanted to be doing, which gave a certain added currency to the old man's beliefs.

The Honourable Member for Qu'Appelle-Gumbo was once a believer as well. He believed in all the years he worked for nothing more than the values of the party. He believed what he said when he knocked on the doors and spoke on the phone and stood in the Elks Lodge and said exactly what he would do for Qu'Appelle-Gumbo when he went to Ottawa for them. He would be their eyes and voice in Parliament; they would be his ears. They would listen to what was being said on Coffee Row and over at the elevator and up at the Lake, and word would come to him, and he would take the word and hammer it into legislation that would fix everything up just the way it should be in a land where the people are good and fair, and the land can be trusted year after year, and the man sent to speak for these good people and this good land damn well knows his job.

Knows his job . . . knows when to shut up and when to stand when he's told and vote what they decide and never, ever, ever let it be known that there might be more than one mind and one common thought locked away in this cold stone building on Parliament Hill. And even this, Tommy reminds himself, is in the past, for it has been months, maybe years now, since the stone building held a thought of any sort, either common or original. The system no longer works. And the country Dominic Sawchuk had believed could somehow use his silver dollar is itself sinking in the muck.

The Honourable T.D.M. Sawchuk knows his thoughts are far too black for Christmas. But what does it really matter what he thinks? He may have come to Ottawa a believer. Now he no longer believes in anything.

Tommy knows he should go for a walk. Clear out the head. Work off the Jos. Louis. Do what he used to do when he was a kid on the farm: go out and stare up into the sky and marvel at the things that cannot be known, rather than stew over what is known. There is no one in the halls. Security does the odd check but everyone else is out of the building. There is no one even staffing the checkpoints. The only sound is the squeak of the Honourable Member for Qu'Appelle-Gumbo's galoshes. In the distance he can hear the Peace Tower bells playing "O Come All Ye Faithful," and he sneers at the irony. He passes the tree in the rotunda and remembers watching Santa Claus hurry by it a week earlier for the staff party. Perhaps this will be the last year for a Santa Claus on Parliament Hill. He is, after all, nearly as politically incorrect as the Honourable Member for Lost Mountain. How much longer can they have a fat, old white guy coming in to the Railway Committee Room to sit little girls and little boys on his lap and offer them, according to gender, dolls and G.I. Joes in exchange for hugs before someone starts up a petition?

The air outside is cold enough to glue your nostrils. But the snow makes it feel warm, and besides, Tommy comes from Saskatchewan and knows what to wear, even if Harry Rosen, instead of the Sears catalogue now does the dressing. There are fat flakes and they slide magnificently out of the light at the back of the Library and down, down, down toward the river. The river is open in the middle, and the lights of Hull bleed in the current. He can see Christmas lights in the apartment towers. To the people who live there, he must be standing in the centre of the most beautiful Christmas scene the country has to offer, but, of course, they cannot see him. No one can clearly see anyone else in this country any more, Tommy thinks, particularly in any view that carries across the Ottawa River in either direction.

He loves to walk among the statues. He likes Laurier and Macdonald and Borden, and he particularly likes the one of John Diefenbaker on the other side of the building, the Chief scowling toward those who arrive for work each day in government cars with government drivers. When the Diefenbakers lived at 24 Sussex Drive, Olive used to mend the curtains. They did Saskatchewan proud.

The Honourable Member for Qu'Appelle-Gumbo has a private member's bill that has been lost in committee, but he still dreams of it one day reaching the floor. It would call for a statue to be raised in memory of Thomas D'Arcy McGee, his namesake. But few know he is his namesake. The other members always ask him if he is related to the old NHL goalie who died in a fight, when, in fact, his connection is to the Father of Confederation who was gunned down on Sparks Street, in another century, on a late April evening, when he stopped to fit his key into the boarding-house lock. He has no way of knowing if he is in fact related, but his mother had a theory that all Irish are related, and that was good enough for her, and it is good enough for him.

The original Thomas D'Arcy McGee would understand what's going on in his country now. When Confederation was being first argued out, the little firebrand called this the "Age of Earthquake," and Tommy Sawchuk is convinced the Age of Earthquake is upon us once again. McGee's obsession was the American civil war. Tommy Sawchuk's belief is that today's Canadian "earthquake" comes out of Tiananmen Square and the Berlin Wall and the fall of the Soviet Union and the sheer utter speed with which everything in this world now moves. The politicians have fallen behind the people. The people have fallen behind the confusion. And for the moment, confusion reigns.

If Tommy's bill would only surface and go through, he would know exactly what to place on the plaque that would grace McGee's statue. The words from the little man's final great speech in the House of Commons, a speech given that April as another province, Nova Scotia, was calling for the repeal of Confederation. "We need above everything else," Thomas D'Arcy McGee told them, "the healing influence of time." Amen to that, says Tommy.

What's moving over there? There is a large flake in Tommy's left eye and he wonders if the blinking has made him think there is someone back of Queen Victoria. He rubs, blinks and looks again. There is someone.

Tommy walks over through the cold snow, and to the right of the statue he stops, watching. Behind the steel fence what appears to be a very old woman is on her knees in the snow. Thinking she is praying, he moves, quietly, for a better look.

But she is not praying. She is feeding a large, yellow cat, which keeps twisting his body against her knees as he turns and eats at the same time. There are other cats, waiting.

Tommy walks to the fence, staring. His galoshes have not warned her.

"Hello," says the Honourable Member for Qu'Appelle-Gumbo.

She does not even turn.

"Hello," he says with more force.

She turns, but not enough, then turns right back to the cats.

"Bon jour," Tommy tries, exhausting a good portion of the knowledge gained from three runs at Berlitz, a two-week stint at a farmhouse in the Gaspé, and more years than he cares to remember when he has pretended he had no need of the earphone during Question Period.

The woman turns, does not smile, but speaks. "Bon soir, monsieur."

Tommy has no idea what to say next. He is used to French-Canadians coming to his rescue. As do the Honourable Member for Lost Mountain and the Honourable Member for Manitou Lake and the Honourable Member for Batoche and a hundred of their colleagues, he knows only the political baby-talk—"Merci, mesdames et messieurs," "La Belle Province," "Mon cher colleague"—and not a damn thing else about a language that is supposed to be as good as his own, whether on Parliament Hill or the Plains of Abraham or, yes, Batoche.

There is nothing to do but struggle and try, and for every small step he dares the old woman takes two, her own smattering of English holding the hand of his pitiful French. But they do talk, and for once, it is talk, in two languages, that has somewhere to go but in circles.

She asks why he is here, and he lies, saying he's leaving later. If he had better control over his French, he would spin the lie to have him picking up some briefing papers before he goes, making some calls, working. He asks what she is doing, and she says nothing, but reaches into one of the bags she carries and pulls up a handful of dried kibble, which she offers to the cat, but it refuses. She offers again, speaking to the cat in an unofficial language that defies translation.

Tommy waits, watching. When she turns briefly into the light, he sees her face, and it is as deeply lined as the drying sides of the slough used to turn in the August sun. There are flakes of snow on her skin. Her eyes are dark and clear. She wears an old camel-hair coat, its texture ground down to the mat in some spots, a tear in the seam where the right arm joins the shoulder. She has a scarf wrapped about her neck, a tartan scarf, but faded. Her hat is rabbit, he thinks, the fur turned inward, but it may, in fact, be fake. Certainly nothing that he would ever have seen in Harry Rosen's or, for that matter, the Sears catalogue.

But more curious than her dress are her bags, two old-style grocery bags of strong manila with jute cord, each one stuffed with white plastic bags, one of which obviously contains kibble. She has her gloves off—children's ski gloves of different designs and colours, as if they came from the bottom of a lost-and-found box—and her bare hands down inside the bags in search of something that is not there.

Tommy asks her if she has lost something, and she says no, she never had what she is looking for, and for a moment Tommy is confused, thinking he has not followed. But she has spoken mostly in English, so he must have understood and he asks more. She says she usually has meat to give them. Sometimes she buys it with her pension, sometimes she brings the scraps she gets from the market butcher shop, sometimes there are leftovers from a restaurant. But tonight, Christmas Eve, there is nothing. She has no money left from her pension. The butcher shop is closed for the holidays. The restaurant shut early and sent everyone home.

There is only kibble, and her hand shakes as she offers it to the yellow tom and the cats that sit waiting beyond. There are now more than a dozen, cats of all colours and cats of all sizes. And in the bare hawthorne bushes there are now squirrels. She digs back down in the bags and comes up with a small handful of peanuts, and the squirrels run to her and climb the old coat onto her shoulder where they stuff themselves from her shaking hand and soon are gone with the nuts, their tracks seemingly too small for their bodies. She digs for more nuts but there are none.

There is nothing left to eat, and nothing left to say. Tommy feels the snow landing again in his lashes and bats the flakes away, blinking some more. He should get back. Maybe make a call. Maybe get one. Get one? Who would know where to find him? But he has to go somewhere.

His toes are freezing. He has on, after all, thin galoshes, not the gumboots he would wear when working around the farm, the farm that hasn't had a Sawchuk drive a combine over it for the better part of a decade, the farm he should be at now. "Home"—even if alone.

He begins backing off, not knowing how to close out this difficult conversation, and she does it for him.

She looks back at him, smiling.

"Joyeux Noël, monsieur."

~~~

The Honourable Member for Qu'Appelle-Gumbo cannot believe what he is doing. He knows he has been back to his office. He knows the bottle of brandy would measure how long he sat there stewing. He knows he has walked down to the ground floor and in through the government lobby and through the green curtains. And he knows, of course, that he is at his desk in the House of Commons, the Honourable Member for Qu'Appelle-Gumbo holding the floor and holding it well.

"I rise, Mr. Speaker," he hears his own voice echoing about the room, "on a matter of urgent and pressing necessity."

Thomas D'Arcy McGee Sawchuk knows that this is no longer done on the floor of the House of Commons, but who is here to check him? He has a statement to make, and more to follow.

"Is it fair, Mr. Speaker, that there are 295 of us in here who have but to snap our fingers and we can move to the front of line for the first-class seats, who can dine daily in one of the most splendid restaurants in the country for a mere pittance, who can park for free, and have our smiling photographs framed for free, and send our mail and make our calls for free, and travel about the world to warm spots when it's cold and come back here and say that this is all work? Is it right that we should have high salaries when so many have no work at all, that we should have indexed pensions when others cannot even afford food for their pets?"

"I suggest not, Mr. Speaker."

And with that, the Honourable Member for Qu'Appelle-Gumbo sits down, but only so long as it takes to pound his desk for old time's sake and shout "Hear! Hear!" toward the empty desk where the *Hansard* reporter would be sitting if it were not Christmas and the House shut down for a month.
~~~

The Honourable Member for Qu'Appelle-Gumbo is on his feet again. "A great Parliamentarian," he says, "and one of our founding Fathers of Confederation, Mr. Speaker, the Honourable Thomas D'Arcy McGee, after whom I am humbly named, once stood in the legislature and told politicians much like us gathered here today that 'the government must lead as well as save, it must march as well as fortify, it must originate plans for the future as well as correct the errors of the past."

"I say to you, Mr. Speaker, that we have lost our way. We cannot lead, we cannot march, we cannot plan, we cannot even act anymore—because we do not know where to go."

"With the permission of the House, then, sir, I ask that my private member's bill pertaining to a suitable monument to this great Canadian be set aside for another time. And instead, Mr. Speaker, I ask that the House now consider a new private member's bill—An Act to Save Our Souls."

The Honourable Member for Qu'Appelle-Gumbo pauses, staring down to where his notes would be if this were a full House—notes prepared by experts and vetted by experts—and he wonders what it would be like to have this much nerve.

"Is the House agreed?" the Speaker asks.

Tommy looks around, but sees no one.

"Yea!"

He looks behind him, to both sides, but sees no one. The shouts seemed to come from every seat.

And then he hears the Speaker's voice again: "The 'yeas' have it."

All these years in Paraliament and Tommy Sawchuk still is not certain how a policy moves from cabinet to legislation, but he knows enough, as most Members do, to get by. Standing alone in the House of Commons with the brandy burning in his stomach and his own gall burning on his face, he carries the bill through three readings, three votes and the Senate. And when it comes time for Royal Assent, he puts it on the record that, since the Governor General is out of the country and no one knows where the Supreme Court justices are holidaying and the Speaker is out of the country and the Prime Minister is out of the country and the cabinet is missing and the House has but one single hard-working Member present, he can therefore give Royal Assent himself, and does so.

But if he does not know exactly how the House works, he certainly knows how the Centre Block functions. At the security check heading into the public galleries he searches for, and finds, the heavy bolt cutters the Hill police keep for the sole purpose of dealing with environmental protesters that chain themselves to barricades. And the bolt cutters, with a few hard twists and deep breaths, get him through the padlocks on the walk-in refrigerator at the rear of the Parliamentary Restaurant.

And now he is pushing a mail cart filled with smoked salmon and pâté and stuffed mushrooms and aged cheeses into the sixth-floor elevator. Now he is on the main floor, pushing the mail cart along the marble corridors, past the subsidized cafeteria to the small hole in the wall where they sell the booze to those who are too lazy and too busy to line up in the stores like everyone else. More work with the bolt cutter—that last twist hurt—and he is inside, a sore hand groping along the bottles for the best that taxpayers' money can buy.

The Honourable Member for Qu'Appelle-Gumbo is laughing now. He has not felt so good since the day he arrived on this Hill, so full of confidence in the system and so certain of what he would do with it. He is acting decisively. In other days he would phone Alice, the moment he had a chance, just to share it with someone who would understand. He would like to phone Alice now. Perhaps he will anyway, later. And not on the government lines, of course. Not even with the extraordinary 24-hour-a-day, seven-days-a-week, 365-days-a-year Privy Council switchboard to track her down. Even if it is about unity.

He is back out in the snow along the west side of the building, and his toes no longer feel cold. The mail cart ruts in the snow and binds, and he wishes he had his father's old team to horse it through. A good push and it gives and slides on, bumping finally into the steel fence.

The old woman is no longer there. But the tom cat is, and one of the squirrels in the tree. The Honourable Member for Qu'Appelle-Gumbo has stuffed his pockets with cashews, and he reaches in and pulls mittfuls free, spewing them over the ground. The squirrel runs for them, and then another black squirrel comes and a red squirrel. They don't know what to make of the nuts. So large, so soft, so sweet. Two nuts and a cheek is full. And Tommy Sawchuk has mittfuls yet to throw.

He brings out the salmon, and the cats come running. He sets out *pâté de foie gras* for them, and they are joined by kittens from a hole under the stone steps. He pours rich cream from silver spouts into china saucers with the Parliament of Canada insignia embossed in gold. He has thin beef cuts and a bowl of shrimp, and when he looks up, he discovers he is surrounded by the animals of the Hill: cats and raccoons and groundhogs, a skunk, squirrels, chipmunks. And the bushes are now filled with birds: chickadees and grosbeak and redpoll and junco, all silently waiting to drop down as the French bread and buns are broken and dumped.

Tommy does not notice the silence, but he starts at the giggle. No animals laugh only the human—and when he turns toward the statue of Victoria, he finds that the old woman is standing behind him, her hands on her bags, her scarf wrapped tight, her face now smiling.

"Joyeux Noël," she says.

"Merry Christmas," the Honourable Member for Qu'Appelle-Gumbo says.

He sees that she is crying. He feels that he is, as well, the streak on his cheek burning with a sensation that takes him back to a wood-frame house at the end of a lane, the smell of the tree, and the sound of the kitchen, and an old man who insisted, no matter the weather, on heading out alone across the field to a small depression in the ground, a single coin in his rough hands.

Thomas D'Arcy McGee Sawchuk doesn't remember when she left. He remembers wrapping half the salmon in her plastic bags and forcing it into her grocery bag. He remembers giving her jars of cashews and plates of pâté. He remembers her saying that she would keep it for the cats. He knows she said she could not take it for herself.

And he remembers that she would have nothing to do with the bottle of cognac he opened. He knows that he himself had been enjoying it, and he remembers searching around in his pocket until he found a loonie—a silly brass dollar that was a poor substitute for the heft and power of a true silver coin—and he knows he walked over to the lookout and threw the loonie as far as he could, hoping it would somehow splash in the open part of the river where the lights of Hull still bled in the current. The coin hurt when it spun off his fingers; it had been years since he had used bolt cutters, and he was paying for it.

He pitched it as far as he could, but heard no splash. And when he came back to the fence, the old woman was gone. He thinks he finished off the bottle.

"Hey, buddy!"

The Honourable Member for Qu'Appelle-Gumbo does not know where he is. He thought he was home for a moment. He thought he was in his office. He thought, for a flash, he was speaking on the floor of the House of Commons. But he was at none of these places. He was cold and he was wet. Very cold. Shaking.

"Are you all right?"

Of course he is all right. And Tommy wants to say so, but can't. He doesn't even know where he is—not yet.

"Mister. Monsieur?"

Where has he heard that before? The old woman, of course—but this is a man's voice. He sees a man now, an older man dressed for winter in a thick parka, an old man with rough hands shaking his shoulders, seeming to want to wake him. Why? From what?

"Leave me alone," the Honourable Member from Qu'Appelle-Gumbo says. "I'm okay."

"Take it easy," the old man says. "Take it easy."

Tommy tries to stand, slips back, and the old man catches him. He is very strong, very sure on his feet. Tommy's own feet feel like boards.

For a long time Tommy stands, leaning against the older man, and the older man waits until Tommy is ready.

"You must have fallen," the older man says.

Tommy looks around. He can see the angel he has left in the snow. He sees, half buried in the fresh snow, the neck of a very expensive bottle of cognac. Cognac . . . Monsieur!

He knows enough to take the obvious out. "I guess I did fall," he says. But he does not know enough to satisfy his bewilderment. "Where is she?" Tommy asks.

"Who? Where is who?"

"The old woman who comes to feed the cats. Where is she?"

"I feed the cats," the older man says.

"You can't."

"I've been coming here every year for four years, my friend. I can and I do. Somebody has to."

"But it was a woman!"

"It was a woman—you're right. But she died four years ago. I do it now."

The Honourable Member for Qu'Appelle-Gumbo has pins and needles in his feet. His head hurts. He can't think clearly.

"But she was here!" he insists.

The older man misunderstands. "She was here, yes. But she died. Did you know her?"

Tommy isn't sure what to say. He knows there must not be talk about him on the Hill.

"No," Tommy says. "Not really."

"You okay now? You want I should call for help?"

"I'm fine. I'm fine, really. But I'm late. I better get going."

"What about this?" the old man asks. "This yours?"

Thomas D'Arcy McGee Sawchuk follows the older man's heavy glove to an old grocery bag, strong manila with a jute cord, white plastic sticking out, pushing through the snow covering.

"It's filled with food," the older man says. "Frozen."

The Honourable Member for Qu'Appelle-Gumbo is as good on his feet as ever. "I brought it for the cats," he says.

"God bless you, mister. And a Merry Christmas to you and yours."

The older man has his glove off and is offering to shake. The politician instinctively reaches for the offered hand, and the old man grips Tommy's soft hand so tightly a blister breaks. Soon there will be calluses.

The Honourable Member for Qu'Appelle-Gumbo smiles through the pain.

"Thanks," Thomas D'Arcy McGee Sawchuk says. "Thanks for your help."

The Christmas Painting

Dominic Ruddick is sitting in church when he begins examining the soul of his truck. Father Scranton—yet another in the long line of student priests sent out from Regina for practise—is droning on about the Christmas spirit and the eternal guiding goodness of the soul, and Dominic simply drifts off and begins thinking about cats and pigeons and snow geese and salmon and snapping turtles and Lucy. His truck, Lucy. And whether or not Lucy has a soul.

Dominic's mind sometimes does that. Given a dry spell—and God knows better than anyone Father Scranton's effect on a congregation—Dominic's mind can scoot like fire over Prairie grass, uncontrollable, unpredictable. The soul is a living entity, says Father Scranton. Lucy seems alive: she talks, she complains, she's started to scream anywhere above 60. The soul has purpose, says Father Scranton. Lucy's trustworthy, she knows her way home so well that Dominic sometimes falls asleep at the wheel, she never fails him.

Dominic once read a story in the big-print *Reader's Digest* about a cat finding its way back home all the way from Toronto to Edmonton. Pigeons have a homing device. Snow geese go back to where they were eggs. Salmon return to the stream where they hatched. His cousin Alf says snapping turtles can be dragged off to another lake and next summer they're right back under the dock . . .

Dominic hates it when his mind runs off like that. Thank God it, too, knows its way home.

"Lovely sermon, Father."

A crazy thing, Dominic thinks, sermons for Christmas. Midnight mass never used to be like this. Midnight mass was ritual, liturgy—Christ's birth the way it should be celebrated, not in some squeaky speech by a kid barely old enough to shave, some student from Regina who thinks all that Africa requires is a full collection plate.

But there is no more midnight mass for Dominic unless he's willing to drive to Saskatoon.

No more Catholic church, for that matter. No more Presbyterian church. No more Lutheran. No more Methodist. Just this catch-as-catch-can Christmas gathering in the Anglican church; Anglicans throwing a holier-than-thou handout to those denominations not founded by a fat king chasing after somebody else's wife.

"Thank you, sir, thank you. Have a very merry Christmas."

He doesn't even know my name, Dominic thinks. Father Schala knew my name, baptized me, confirmed me, buried my father, and helped me move mother into the home. Now he's dead.

His church is empty. There used to be 11 churches in Brimstone, now there's one, this one. There are more people in the graveyard today than in the town. Dominic counted them up himself last summer: dead 483, alive 391. And in the four months since, Dominic figures, he could shift another four from one column to the other—and remove another nine for the two young families that left for Moose Jaw just before school started.

There have been more people leaving Brimstone than coming in now for 20 years. You pick up your mail at the gas station. You truck your wheat up to Newcome. The tracks are overgrown, the member of parliament has hands as soft as a piglet's belly, there're salt patches all over the back quarter . . .

Come back, brain—there's still the drive home.

"Thank you, father. You, too."

Dominic stands alone for awhile in the church parking lot. It is still snowing heavily. The headlights look through heavy, pale lids of cover, so dim they seem as if they're dying. Some drivers have barely bothered to cuff a porthole on the driver's side of the windshield and they're off, front-wheel drive, all-season radials quiet as slippers as they move away from him and down toward the Main Street turn.

It used to take Dominic a good hour to get away from mass, a good—a wonderful—hour of standing around stomping his feet and talking about the Leafs and complaining about the Wheat Board payments. Now they race for their cars and the heat, and run for home. Afraid of a little snow. Some of them even have little gizmos hanging from their sun visors that they push and the garage door opens automatically. Push again and it shuts the door. Lucy doesn't even have a garage. No radials, either, or front-wheel drive, but tire chains that Dominic oils and packs in burlap every spring for every fall. No heat either, for that matter.

But she does know her way home.

~~~

Dominic had come down to The Thrasher at 10:15 that morning. No one, not even Dominic, had checked the old Pool clock over the cash; no one had to.

He'd come in to Coffee Row every morning since 1973 at 10:15. He never even thought about it. It was simply when he got there, or when Lucy got him there.

The boys were already well into their second cups. Milt Arnell, Danny Latch, Wilf Payette, Lonnie and Gil, the Dirk brothers. Each arriving at his precise minute, each sitting in his usual seat. The only things that ever changed were the caps and the smoke. Caps wore out; the Dirk brothers quit smoking the day a pack of cigarettes cost more than a bushel of wheat, and the higher tobacco prices went, the more smokers dropped off; now no one smoked unless Dominic counted in Milt who sometimes chewed.

Dominic loved the drive in from the old farmhouse. Three and a half miles to come up with an opener. He'd have it by the time Lucy made it over the old railroad tracks, he'd say it two or three times out loud by the time she turned into The Thrasher. He'd say it quietly to himself as he walked up to the door, placed a hand on the knob, and a foot on the base in winter, and popped it open into a faceful of heat, a noseful of coffee and an earful of his own name.

"Dommie's here."

"Hey Dom, whatya got for us this morning?"

"Nothin'." Always that: Nothin'. With a smile.

"Come on."

Okay: "Wilf, you're so old now you have to fantasize *you're* someone else when you're makin' love."
~~~

Not his best, but the laughter as warm and familiar as that first blast of heat when the door opened. All part of the ritual. Dominic's opener, the laughter, the head shaking, the spoon stirring as Dominic sits down in precisely the same spot and Marilyn plops down the heavy white cup of coffee, three creams and a spoon. Five sugar cubes, a sip while it's still hot enough to burn, and Coffee Row was under way for another morning. Just as always.

But Dominic knew that the very thing that never changes was changing, even if no one ever mentioned it. Dougall Grizzard used to be sitting right there between Danny and Lonnie. Now, he'd moved to the more populous part of town, the cemetery. Downwardly mobile, Dominic called it in one of his more regrettable openers, but the point he was trying to make was spot on: they were slowly dying off. According to the world's biggest gossip, Dr. Kristich, who held a clinic every Thursday in Doc Kluzak's old offices, Wilf wasn't at all well himself.

The townspeople were going the same way as the town, Dominic was convinced. Some were shutting down, some moving away, most avoiding the obvious. Milt walked poorly; the Co-op he ran needed a new roof, new paint, new customers. Mrs. Brighton—Marilyn's mother—needed a hip operation and had emphysema; The Thrasher, the highway restaurant her no-good husband left her with, needed a new kitchen, new underground tanks for the gas, new china. Everyone and everything was beginning to crumble.

"How's your mum?" Wilf asked when Dominic's second cup of coffee arrived at the usual time without being ordered.

"Oh, pretty much the same."

Dominic liked them to ask, even if she was always pretty much the same. They asked, knowing the answer, just as Dominic always asked after Wilf's son, Barry, who was still down in the minor leagues hoping to get the call-up from the Leafs. Cargill was more likely to come to town and build a new grain elevator. Canadian Pacific was more likely to build a new spur into town for passenger service. Wheat was more likely to hit $10 a bushel. But he always asked anyway.

At noon, with three cups of coffee, the soup of the day and a grilled-cheese sandwich in his belly, Dominic headed for the senior citizen's residence. Lucy got him there just when they were clearing away the dishes. Just as always.

His mother had been eating with Mrs. Castnor and that old woman from over Yorkton way whose name neither Dominic nor his mother could ever remember.

Mrs. Castnor used a walker and was heading off, determined to do it alone. The old woman from over Yorkton way was complaining, as usual, about the way the nurse kept ignoring her so. Dominic and his mother did precisely as the nurse always did, ignored her and walked way.

They always went back to sit and talk in her room—a nice little room with her own bed, the old dresser from the farm, her crewel work, photos of Dominic's father, gold-framed family portraits of the girls and their shining families in Winnipeg and Regina, and, on the wall, framed and labelled, the old photo of the homestead, circa 1952.

Those were the best years. In 1952, Dominic's father's business was taking off, literally. A farmer who became an RCAF pilot in the war, he had come back to Saskatchewan and leased the farm to Orville Payette, Wilf's dad; then he took out a bank loan and bought a used, single-engine Stinson from a bush pilot up north of Prince Albert. Dominic's mother said he'd gone mad from too much of that French wine. But he said he had an idea that couldn't fail, and it didn't. After he got the plane he bought a fancy camera, took photography lessons down in Regina, and then taught Dominic how to use it while he flew the old Stinson all across the province, banking the plane like a snow goose, while the boy leaned out the window and snapped a shot of every farm they could locate on the grid maps. They got the shots developed and drove around the dusty, rutted back roads knocking on doors and showing people what God saw when he looked down at their homestead. Near as Dominic could ever figure, nine out of every 10 farms bought—even if they couldn't afford it.

The real secret to success came in the '50s, though. Dominic's father figured they'd pretty well covered the market and was thinking about going into crop dusting when his wife came up with the idea of painting the pictures.

Dominic's mother had always fiddled with painting and other fancy-work. It sold well at the church bazaars, but no one ever figured she could make real money at it. She painted a few to see, one of them of their own farm, the one that now hangs in her bedroom at the seniors' residence, and the effect was astounding. She painted the trees green, the wheat fields golden, put a little purple over the quarter where they'd put in rape—it looked just like it was coming into bloom—touched up the old farmhouse with a bit of white, blackened the barn, put a dot of red over the tractor, and the photograph looked as if it had been shot in CinemaScope.

No one could believe it. Dominic's father couldn't believe how cheap it was to do. And not only could he charge double the price, he could sell the shots all over again to the farmers who'd bought back in '47 and '48. He immediately bought a new Cessna 150—a bit lighter, easier to slow for shutter speed and sharper focus—and began all over again.

The business took the family right through to the old pilot's death in 1979, the same year Dominic—who'd never flown legally, never bothered with a licence, and hated the way the Cessna kept cutting out on him and stalling when he banked too sharply—sold the business to Alex Kraftchik over by Highway 6, and took over working the quarters they'd been leasing out to the Payettes for as long as anyone could remember. Three years later, Kraftchik was out of business, beaten to the ground by ridiculous satellite photographs from space and helicopter shots and soaring interest rates and the inescapable truth that the farms in Saskatchewan would never again look as magnificent and inviting as when Dominic's mother was touching them up after the fact.

Every day Dominic sat for an hour with his mother. They would have tea together, and Dominic's mother would wander. She was getting worse, much worse, but it didn't bother Dominic. Often she thought her husband was still alive. She always talked about the airplane like it was still tied down in the field. She talked about townspeople now dead and buildings now torn down and abandoned. She sometimes thought she was at church and repeated, word for word, the epistle as Father Schala would lead them through it.

She would talk about box socials and baseball games from the 1930s as if they had just been held that afternoon. She would ask him if there was enough wood cut for the school, and he could smell the sawdust when he'd take an armful, kick open the pot belly and fire it up for Miss Amberwood, who'd come out from Ontario and was still in town as Mrs. Gil Dirk. She'd talk about the bulls Dominic would show and remember their names and placings. She'd talk about the day Tommy Douglas came to town and spoke at the Methodist church and how they, good Catholics, had gone anyway. She'd talk about the Red and White store and the livery and Chester Bullock, the drayman, and the butcher's, talk about the day rich Mr. Percival's new Case runabout arrived by rail and no one could figure out how to start it, talk about Kitty McAlpine's bridge parties and Carl Brodeur's pool hall and even complain about the dogs—by name—that were running loose along Main Street.

Sometimes, if it was warm enough and he had nothing better to do, Dominic would actually encourage his mother to drift off by asking her about someone he hadn't thought about for 40 years or more, and then, while she began with a name and flew off into an era, he'd drift off himself, his eyes closed, his mind filling up again with a better time.

The good old days, painted even better than they originally looked.

~~~

"Goodnight, goodnight, goodnight, Father. Merry Christmas, Merry Christmas, Merry Christmas . . ."

Dominic wishes they held the midnight service at noon, so he could take his mother. She would enjoy this, but it's just too late for her. She would love the snow and the way it tickles on your eyelashes when you look up. She would love the lightness of it as Dominic knocks the snow off the cab with the old broom that's been stiff as a board now for years. She would love the sound of the chains as Lucy heads out of the parking lot and off toward the highway, the chains softly ringing as Lucy heads left while the other vehicles all turn right, right with everyone else to bring them to their homes in town, left alone to the old elevator road and the back way home.

The back way: Dominic sometimes wonders if he could even go the other way anymore, it has been so long. He stopped using the main highway the week they moved the RCMP detachment out of Brimstone and back down the road to Carefree. He no longer knew the Mounties on patrol. They no longer knew him. And considering the state of Lucy—no horn, no tail lights, no turn signals, the emergency brake lying on the seat beside him, high beams only, brakes pulling to the right, enough play in the wheel she sometimes felt like a boat in rough water, suspension gone, shocks dead, heater broken—he didn't dare go the highway so long as there was still life and oil and gas in Lucy.

The back way takes him past the shell of the old Pool elevator, past the shell of the old train station where the CPR once stopped automatically, where for awhile it stopped only if you called ahead, where it eventually stopped stopping at all and then, finally, stopped even running. The back way takes him past the cemetery, past the old abandoned Duncan place, down along Payette's quarter, along the original Ruddick quarter and then in the lane to the old farm.
~~~

It has snowed more than Dominic figured. It must have come down hard during the service for he can barely make out the two thin sags in the road where he himself had come out to church—what?—only two hours earlier. And it is blowing now, the snow suddenly lurching up from the ditches like a frightened deer, momentarily blanking out the windshield. And Lucy with no heater.

Dominic hates moments like this. His own breath is steaming up the inside of the windshield, the sudden tossed blankets of snow cover the outside; it is just warm enough inside the cab to lock the bursts of snow onto the outside. He has to drive with the window down to take away the inside steam, and then stick his arm out with the scraper to keep the outside clear enough to see. Thank God Lucy knows her way home.

Dominic wishes he had low beams. The high beams are too strong, too high, and they bounce back at him in the snow that is now falling even harder.

It makes him feel like Lucy is floating. He can no longer see his marks. He can no longer feel the road.

When Lucy first bottoms, he can't believe it. He feels the lurch—bangs his arm hard against the no-draft—and thinks for a moment Lucy must have struck a coyote. He presses the accelerator but cannot hear the chains. Only the sizzle of the truck engine as the snow that bounced up when Lucy went off the road melts on the engine block. Dominic turns off the engine and, for a moment, is shocked by the sound: the sound of a kettle of cold water being poured over a red-hot wood stove, the sound of trouble.

He can hear the snow itself out the window, can hear the wind, as well. But he can see nothing. He does not even know where he is. He has travelled this same road thousands of times and yet cannot say precisely where he has bogged down. He can see no landmark, only a tight wrap of falling snow and the truck and the flat, slightly higher ridge where, presumably, the road runs. The road home. The road Lucy knows by heart.

Dominic gets out and surveys the situation, though there is little to learn from getting out. He reaches back in, turns off the high beams, but can see nothing, even when he turns in a full circle. The snow is over his knees. He has no winch. No one will be coming along.

For the first time in years—the first time, probably, since the engine of the little Cessna last cut out on him—Dominic feels panicky. He can barely see the road.

He knows no one could walk far in snow this deep. He knows there is no heater in Lucy. Lucy is supposed to know the way home.

Dominic remembers his father stringing up a rope between the shed and the barn every December, a rope just in case. He could make his way to the shed off the summer kitchen, then the rope would guide him to the barn if it was snowing too hard to see. He only needed the line maybe one day out of every five or six winters, but at least the animals got fed, and he got there and back. Everyone, it seemed, had a story of a disoriented farmer freezing to death within shouting distance of home.

Dominic knows better than to let panic control him. He steps back into the cab, sits for a moment, then checks Lucy's vital signs. More than half full. He can run her and turn the high beams back on. And there'll be heat from the engine, even if hardly any of it can find its way back along the vents. He starts the engine, turns on the lights and gets out to assess the damage.

He is not as far off the road as feared. By walking all around Lucy he finds he has footing everywhere, so it is not a deep ditch. The way is clear back onto the road if he can go in reverse, so if he can just dig out the rear and the front where the wheels will have to turn, then the chains should be able to haul him back up. He could, if necessary, go all the way back to town in reverse. Lucy knows the way.

But he has nothing but the broom for digging. Nothing but a damn broom when there was a time Dominic would carry a complete tool kit in the back including two shovels—in case one handle breaks—a small winch, a cable and an axe. He has let things slide. Everything has been let slide.

The snow is light though, and the broom is still enough for clearing. Dominic goes to work and in 15 minutes is sweating. He begins to believe in himself again. He could, if necessary, work all night and be warm as toast and someone would come along in the morning or else, in the daylight, he could walk home. He knows the way, too.

And the snow is letting up. It is hardly falling at all now. And Dominic can see breaks in the sky off toward the north. So there is hope.

Dominic digs and pushes and works for more than an hour. He is soaking wet with sweat now, and when he gets into the cab to start up again and try the chains, he shivers. The chains sing as he lets out the clutch, sing and then chunk as they catch, then bounce free and sing again. Double-clutching and shifting fast between first and reverse, Dominic tries to rock Lucy and bounce her out. The truck heaves forward, then back, then forward, back, forward, back, then slips hard sideways, deeper down into the drift.

Dominic gets out to check. The truck is going nowhere, nowhere at all. Lucy is in deeper, the one rear wheel riding high and useless over the snow, the other hammered down so tight, and the snow has plugged the wheel well and stalled anything from moving.

He is stuck.

Dominic feels colder now, much colder. He is shivering, shaking. He knows there is no more use shovelling with the broom. He knows he will never get Lucy out on his own.

He has two choices: he can start walking or he can get back into the cab and try to preserve what heat he can. If only he'd been better prepared. If only he'd fixed the heater instead of letting it go. The big-print *Reader's Digest* had a story about an elderly couple surviving an avalanche in their car with nothing for heat but a single candle and a can, but he didn't even have that, didn't even have a match. If he stays, he will freeze. He has no real choice but to walk.

The snow lies in waves. Sometimes it is as high as Dominic's hips, sometimes as low as the top of his boots. Light when he knocked it off the windshield, it is now heavy, and he is sweating again, but instead of feeling warm when he sweats, the dampness is cold, frightening.

The sky is clear now. There is no sound to the snow, no sound to the wind. No wind, in fact, only the distant howl of a train whistle.

Dominic stops. A train? What train? There has been no train through here in years; there are no tracks for 40 miles. But it is that sound and there—off back of the Duncan lights in the distance—there is the sweep of the train light. Dominic can even make out the plume of smoke, white as cloud in the navy sky. CP 407 due in at 1:58, dead on time.

Dominic knows he is wandering. It is the cold. He read about hypothermia once in the big-print *Reader's Digest* and how disorientation is one of the signs. He must concentrate; he must not wander.

The train grows louder as it approaches. He can see sparks now in the plume, sparks along the tracks and in one frightening, screaming blast the train vanishes back of the Duncan barn and is gone.

The Duncan barn? But it caved in 30 years ago. The boards are in half the basements in town. And lights at the Duncan place?

There is another sound now, fainter, smaller, almost like an electric razor. But as it grows it becomes more familiar to Dominic. It is a sound he has not heard for decades. It is the distinctive, distant hum of a Stinson aircraft coming in low.

Dominic stops, his breath now coming in quick gulps, his breath escaping with every drum slap of his heart. He can not only hear the Stinson, he can see it. High over the community pastureland to the west, heading up from the runway along the edge of the original quarter. He can see its flying lights, red and green and white, blinking in the distance, regular as Christmas light bulbs.

The plane comes directly overhead and dips its wings—He sees me!—and then banks sharply to starboard, just as Dominic's father always did when he came back home, a wing tip to put supper on: he'd be in, and hungry, in less than an hour, the plane tied down, the film out of the camera and ready to be sent off to Winnipeg for processing.

The film! He can't shoot himself! Dominic looks as the plane banks and watches it cut across the moon: two figures, one tall, one short and behind. His father and his helper. Me!

Dominic stares down at the ground and shakes his head. He grabs a mittful of snow and rubs his face in it. He is dying from hypothermia. But the sound is still there, the plane is still in the sky, and they are passing directly over the old Duncan place and then banking so sharp the plane practically stalls. The moment Dominic would snap the photograph.

The plane banks again and then is gone, headed back over the fields and then dipping down toward the original quarter runway and home.

Silence now—and then, while Dominic stands staring, his mouth open and the cold drilling his teeth—the scene in front begins to lighten and take on colour. First the old barn, the roof bleeding red and gleaming in the black-and-white night. Then the house, now washing white, new glass in the windows, a Christmas tree behind sheer curtains, candles everywhere.

The light moves like one of the spotlights Dominic used to operate during the Christmas recitals at the church, its border sharp enough to feel as it moves out across the yard and on toward the far outline of the town.

And as the light moves, Brimstone comes back to Dominic. The grain elevators, dark green for Cargill, bright yellow for the Pool. The little train station rises, green with red trim, and a light comes on inside, and suddenly he realizes that the reason the train whistle had stopped is because the train, too, has stopped. And there is life around the cars, people getting off. People coming to Brimstone.

The town itself brightens and takes on colour. The John Deere yard fills with machinery. Wilf's Co-op brightens, a new sign shining into the night. No, the old sign—but the way it was before the kids put the rocks through it. And there—sticking up into the night with electric lights on it—the Catholic Church steeple! And all the other churches, back, alive, packed with supplicants for the Christmas service.

"You need some help?"

Dominic spins in the snow. There is a man there, and a boy. He does not know them.

"You okay, mister?"

Dominic tries to speak but cannot. His mouth feels frozen, his lips wooden blocks. He decides instead to go to them and lifts his right leg to step. But it will not move either. Dominic rocks once, then falls face first straight into the snow his vision suddenly black, his face stinging as it plunges into the snow.

~~~

His nose awakens first. Locked shut by the cold the last time he tried, his nostrils now fill with smells as comforting as the words his mother sometimes uses when she wanders. Coal oil and wood fire, the pungent-sweet smell of wool drying, lye soap, a kettle of water slowly steaming, the smell of soup from scratch, the smell of pine, of candles, of Christmas.

He opens his eyes and the faces are floating above him. No, he is lying down, lying on a sofa in a very warm room. The boy is staring down at him. He seems to be speaking and then there is a woman staring down and a girl, all worried.

"Are you all right?" the woman asks.

"Where am I?" Dominic asks.

"We're the Duncans. Who might you be?"

"Dominic Ruddick."

"There's a child up the road by that name—you related?"
~~~

Dominic cannot follow, cannot answer. The woman speaks for him. "You should eat."

The girl is setting a place at the table. She is carrying soup to a place set for one. With help, Dominic gets up, and finds his feet are in heavy woollen socks, someone else's socks. It is his own clothes drying that he has smelled. He looks up and his socks and pants and coat are hanging off binder twine strung between the stove-pipes and the wall. His pants are steaming.

"Daniel says you'd have frozen to death in another half-hour."

"Daniel?"

"Mr. Duncan. My husband. He's taken the team out to pull your rig free."

"There's no sign of your horse," the boy says.

"It's run off. Father says we'll go out looking in the morning."

Dominic is too tired to argue, too tired to ask. He smells the soup and in a moment he is sitting and tasting it, and he is thinking about turnips and leeks and ham bones, and wondering how it is that he has not tasted such delight since he was a child. The girl is putting tea on the table—thick, black tea with leaves spinning in it—and the boy is carrying a plate of thick shortbread and placing it down beside the tea.

"Mom made this for Christmas. She says you get to try it first."

Dominic tries it and the shortbread bursts in his mouth, butter and sugar—real sugar, not that refined, bleached junk he drops in his coffee down at The Thrasher. It is so sweet and rich he wishes he could chew forever, wishes he could sit and eat and cry like a baby if only they weren't all standing there staring at him.

"Well?" the boy says.

"John." the mother snaps.

Dominic smiles. "The best I've ever had. Ever."

The moment breaks with the spring of the front door and the rush of winter. The farmer comes in backwards, quickly closing the door and shouldering it shut. He stomps his feet, claps his heavy leather mitts and begins peeling off winter while he talks, his breath made short by the exertion and the bitter cold.

"You're out, Mister. Took two good horses and a poor man, but you're out."

"Can I get up the road?"

"We'll find out in the morning, mister. You stay here with us tonight. We'll wait till morning."

Wilf Payette heard it first. A distant sound he caught when he let out the dog and at first ignored, but when he let the barking dog back in and the dog, wouldn't stop barking, he stepped into his boots, went out and turned the corner of the house, and heard it louder, coming from over Dominic Ruddick's way.

Wilf didn't realize what it was till he and his son-in-law turned into the lane at Ruddick's and saw where Dominic's old truck had plowed through the drifts like a train with a plow attached.

The two men couldn't believe a truck could make it through them; some of the drifts were up past the wheel wells and their four-wheel drive could barely follow Dominic's tracks. And Dominic's old heap was rear-wheel drive only.

"Maybe it's the chains," Wilf's son-in-law suggested.

Wilf said nothing. He now knew what the sound was: a horn.

Up ahead they could see Lucy bogged down right in front of the old house, and Dominic slumped straight forward over the steering wheel. His chest must have set off the horn—Wilf thought he remembered Dominic calling the Co-op just last week to see if he had one in stock—and somehow the horn hadn't yet run down the battery.

Wilf must have described this scene to a dozen people by the time the ambulance finally got here from Saskatoon. "Damn lucky thing he fell that way," Wilf told them all. "Hadn't a been for the horn he'd a froze to death."

As it was, Dominic had a bad case of frostbite. The medic also talked about hypothermia, said Dominic was wandering, talking about airplanes and a man and a team and there was nothing for anyone to concern themselves about, he'd be fine in a few hours. They'd take him to Saskatoon just to make sure.

Most of the gang from Coffee Row had come out. News travels fast in a small town, even on Christmas Day. Father Scranton, the young Anglican priest, came along after the morning service and said he was coming out to the Ruddick place anyway—but never would have arrived in time. "Thank the Lord", he said, "Wilf had heard the horn."

Father Scranton said he'd go with the ambulance up to Saskatoon.

He'd wait until the doctors checked Dominic over first.

"And then I'm afraid I'll have to tell him about his mother."

The Christmas Spoon

Clarence Brody felt like throwing up—but he knew he could not, must not. He knew what would happen once the story got back to Waapikun. Another example of how weak he was. Another little titbit for them to snicker over behind his back. Another brick in the wall that had steadily been going up between Clarence and the villagers since he came to help—what was it now?—two years ago come spring. Two years . It seemed like a lifetime ago. And the way this plane was bouncing through the sky, it very well might be just exactly that.

The old Fokker was high over the Northern Quebec taiga and dropping down through broken cloud and air pockets. It fell, bumped, yanked sideways, levelled out, collapsed, bumped again and fell again helplessly, Clarence Brody hanging onto his breakfast buffet as tightly as the other passengers gripped their breakable Christmas presents. No one said anything: not the pilots, not the stewardess who had given up trying to find her footing after 10 minutes of moving around like a heavy diver on a floating dock, certainly not Clarence and none of the dozen or so others, all of them Cree, all of them heading home from a shopping binge in Val-d'Or where, it seemed to Clarence, they had all spent far too foolishly and far too excessively. As far as he was concerned, Christmas in James Bay was another threatening megaproject.

The plane bucked again. Bucked—exactly the word—for Clarence had not felt such a face-shifting disorientation since the Preservation Club won its clear-cutting blockade out in British Columbia and all headed off to celebrate at the Williams Lake rodeo, where he'd had too many beer and ended up being thrown by the mechanical bull. Thank God no one here knew that story; there were already enough.

Below the clouds now, the plane shimmied and settled, the relief instantaneous. Conversations that had been put on hold while minds dealt with death were picked up without the slightest hint that speaker or listener had been promising God their next-born if only. The stewardess clicked off her seat belt and went back to the rear of the plane. Clarence discreetly tucked the air-sickness bag back into the seat and turned his attentions to the window, staring hard at nothing.

It always struck him odd when he said that. There's nothing up there. There's nothing out there. Some found beauty in the North; they said they loved the barrenness, they loved the way you could look down from a plane and feel that if anything moved below, you would catch it, but nothing had ever moved when Clarence was staring down, ever. Others told him they loved the way it stayed light so long in the summer up here, and stayed faintly bright even in the winter because of the snow and village lights. They said they loved the way the northern lights could ripple like a sheet being aired out. What could move them like that? Clarence was convinced it was the wind: if it could blow that hard, it could blow that high. He hated the north wind. Always blowing. Always blowing cold. Always bringing bad news. A storm coming. The geese not coming. Hunters lost on the bay . . . The wind was the only thing he knew for certain was out there—and wind he could not see. Nothing.

They passed low over the Whitefish river, the rapids boiling white and tinted yellow against the ice that had formed on the deeper, slower parts of the river. Clarence had never been on the Whitefish, but the Whitefish was his all the same. The Preservation Club had funded his work on the Whitefish, Gerald Parlor's work on the Nottaway, Paul Desjardin on the Broadback, Missy Finebender on the Rupert and the work of four environmentalists on Great Whale, which the Club had precious little hope now of saving. It had already gone too far. The Preservation Club's strategy insofar as the Whitefish project or the Nottaway, Broadback and Rupert projects were concerned was to ensure that the situation never reached the negotiation stage. What mattered was blocking this as surely and effectively as the Club had blocked the logging trucks heading up into the B.C. interior. But here there would be no lying down in front of huge, mud-caked wheels; blocking would be through hard research. Clarence's assignment was to gather material for what many in the Club felt would be the most striking argument: cultural genocide. Public opinion would lie down in front of these trucks, and they would never make first gear.

Sometimes his assignment baffled Clarence Brody. He was to gather oral histories and empirical data to demonstrate the need for preservation steps to be taken. He was to show that there would be environmental damage, and obviously there would be, but his research was also to demonstrate that development money, from New York State and New Jersey and Vermont and, for that matter, Montreal, was doing more damage than good in the North. And here is where he ran into trouble.

Which argument, for example, would Christmas favour? The celebration had been brought here by the missionaries, and it was possible to look at the missionary work as an early megaproject, and distant collection plates as original development money. According to the anthropologists who'd been to Waapikun in the summer, the Cree had been here, settled and happy, long before Christ was even born—so what was the point of Clarence pining for a traditional Christmas in the North as opposed to a Val-d'Or shopping spree or, worse, the panic buying that had been taking place all December long on the shopping channel beamed into the village by satellite? There was no gasoline sniffing before the first megaproject, and none obviously, as well, before the first priests came paddling down the Whitefish.

Clarence's challenge was to show how the real flooding of James Bay—by southern culture and southern money—had destroyed a way of life over the past two decades. There had already been hundreds of millions of dollars come in, and now they were talking about hundreds of millions more. They were recycling trouble: more money, more desire, more consumption, more anguish. It seemed impossible to stop.

Clarence had always found that Christmas befuddled him. He had been born in Ottawa in 1947, nine months, he once calculated, after the release of *It's a Wonderful Life*. He had been named after the guardian angel who talks Jimmy Stewart out of killing himself by showing him how everything would have turned out differently if he had not been put on earth. In other words, there was a purpose.

But what, pray, was Clarence's? He had gone to school, marched against the Vietnam War, voted NDP, written a thousand letters to get people out of jail, stood vigil for the loss of agricultural land, distributed flyers on the disappearance of the ozone layer and—if truth be told—arrived at the B.C. blockade about three hours after the forestry company decided to pull out and pack it in. In other words, a fairly convincing argument could be put up that if Clarence Brody had never entered this world, not a damn thing would have changed. He hated the movie.

And yet, here he was, assigned by the Preservation Club to be the guardian angel to a society that didn't much care for him. The Cree were usually polite to him, just as Jimmy Stewart had been to his Clarence, but the movie character had spent a lot more time listening and thinking in two hours than the Cree had in two years. They found him lodgings and answered his questions, but then confounded the usual act of dealing through an interpreter.

It irritated Clarence Brody that he could ask a simple question, his paid interpreter would spend more than a minute repeating the question to one of the older Cree, they'd laugh wildly at each other, and then the interpreter would turn and give him a flat, one-sentence answer. He didn't have to wonder if they were talking about him. All he had to do was listen.

He talked to them about the importance of preserving their language, and they talked back to him in Cree, laughing. He talked to them about preserving the traditional pursuits like hunting, and they asked him if he wanted to come with them on their new Ski-Doo and try out their brand-new five-shell pump-action shotgun. Clarence was beginning to believe the battle had already been lost.

Perhaps he should have bailed out the first day he flew into Waapikun. It was at the end of August and he had looked out of the rattling old Otter as it began its approach and he had seen a bulldozed road leading in to a clearing blanketed with snow. Perhaps, he had thought at the time, this is where the village gets its name, waapikun—white feather. But when he asked about the snow when the plane landed, the pilots had laughed at him. "What you saw were Pampers," they said. "That's the dump."

~~~

Now another plane, two years later, was dipping down toward the same gravel runway; half-tons and four-wheel-drive Jeeps and snowmobiles were already heading out in the half-light of mid-afternoon to meet the passengers and carry the presents back to the homes. Enough money spent on gifts, Clarence Brody figured, to finance three or four years of his work. Work , he smiled. Is work without product work or waste? Heading into a new year, Clarence Brody did not feel particularly hopeful.
~~~

They had put Clarence up in Lanny Smoke's home. Lanny was a hunter who spent most of the winter in the bush, most of the summer netting and smoking fish along the Whitefish, most of the fall and most of the spring at a goose camp two terrifying hours up the coast by Hudso Bay canoe and 25-horse Mercury at full throttle. Clarence had gone once. He threw up on the way up. He thought he was going off to see a traditional Cree hunting camp, soft balsam boughs on the ground and spruce for the walls and roof, the cracks chinked with fur or mud. Instead, he found a permanent hut made of planed framing wood wrapped with orange plastic tarpaulin. Lanny brought a battery-operated four-inch colour television with him so he could watch the hockey play-offs. And Clarence threw up again on the way back.

Clarence had no idea what to make of Lanny. He talked of leading the traditional life, but he did so on the Cree hunting plan, which required him to stay in the bush a certain number of days per year to qualify for the guaranteed-income scheme. In other words, Lanny Smoke was on a per diem the moment he headed away from his village home.

With Lanny gone most of the time, the house was left to Beulah, his wife, and Lanny's mother, Ruth, who was in her 80s and worked most of the day on patchwork quilts the Cree then sold at the store they ran down in Val-d'Or. Traditional native patchwork quilts. Traditional native Singer-sewn dresses. Traditional native satellite dishes. Clarence was getting negative. He knew he would have to fight it.

On the Wednesday before Christmas there was to be a combination Christmas pageant at the school and a brief update on the situation regarding the hydro company and the Whitefish river. Clarence was slated to speak.

He had walked over alone—always alone, the black dogs sniffing and growling alongside him—and he was grateful to hear the priest calling his name as he turned off Lanny Smoke's road and headed down the hill toward the water. He had often felt, if he ever slipped, he was doomed. Down south it might mean a knee thrown out; up here it might mean a throat ripped out.

Father Boudrias was breathless when he arrived.

"You invited to the big feast?" the priest asked.

"What feast?"

"Tomorrow night," the priest seemed irritated. "I'm not either. Someone mentioned it after church—I don't know anything more than that about it."

Someone? Clarence wondered why he wouldn't just say Old Jack Shaapumin told him? Father Boudrias had been reduced to serving high mass for a congregation of one for nearly a year now, the village having left en masse, so to speak, for the two fundamental churches that had come into the community. According to Old Jack, the priest still poured as much communion wine as ever; further, Old Jack added, he himself barely got to touch his lips to the chalice. Clarence didn't know what to believe. Was it true? Or was it just another story to turn the outsiders into the village idiots?

Clarence did not seem as upset as the priest over the lack of invitation. Why would he be invited? Why would he even care? He was supposed to be back in Ottawa, anyway, but the Club claimed it was so strapped for money, thanks to the recession and the costs of fighting B.C. timber companies, that all workers were down to two trips home a year, and Clarence had a family wedding in April and a cottage on the Rideau booked for August. Besides, he had tapes to transcribe.

Together they walked up the steps of the school, the hot, stale air and sharp noise pushing against their faces as the door gave and they entered. No one paid them the slightest heed as they shed their heavy coats and boots, and walked, in sock feet, into the gymnasium where they took seats near the back. The smell of smoke was overwhelming. Not cigarette smoke, but the smell of fire smoke hanging off clothes and hair. He had smelled the geese hanging in the cooking tents on the way over. He should have known there was a feast coming.

The pageant was put on by the grade-eight class and absolutely baffled both the priest and Clarence and infuriated the school principal, a thin, nervous man near the end of his assignment. The story was the nativity tale, but told in the Cree language in a bush setting. (Clarence wondered why the stable wasn't made out of orange plastic tarpaulin.) The children were charming and some were very good with their lines, but the entire class—as well as the audience—kept breaking up and twice could not go on for several minutes. Both times the principal had darted up the steps and angrily brought them to order by snapping his fingers at the worst snorters. He didn't dare try the same disciplinary measure with the crowd. Clarence had no idea what was going on. Clarence spent the time of the play carefully going over the mental notes of what he would say.

Some of the children left at the end of the school play. Others stayed. First, the Chief of Waapikun, Lucy Stringer, a tall, soft-featured woman with a strong voice, spoke in both languages, but mostly Cree, on the state of the projects and what was going on within the Cree nation. She talked of a letter-writing campaign under way in New York and Vermont, and a private member's bill in parliament that held some promise, and then she turned the proceedings over to Clarence, who was introduced as a great friend of the Waapikun band. No one applauded as Clarence made his way up and took the microphone.

Clarence explained his current project and, from time to time, Chief Lucy Stringer spoke in Cree. Clarence had to presume she was interpreting, but the laughing bothered him. For all he knew, she could be saying anything she wished about him. He wished that he, like the principal, could merely snap his fingers at them and they would smarten up and pay attention. He talked about the interviews he wanted to do with all the village elders, and how he particularly wanted them to tell him how it had been before the arrival of money and airplanes and television. He tried to tell them all how vital this would be to any presentation the Preservation Club might make to the various levels of government and the media.

"Excuse me!" someone shouted.

With the light on him, Clarence had difficulty making out who was speaking. He came to an abrupt halt and stood there, waiting. Finally a young man pushed his way through the crowd and stood facing Clarence, who could hear nothing but his own heart pounding inside his ears. The young man was Arnold Whiskeyjack, who had run, and lost, against Lucy Stringer in the last band election for chief.

"Are we to take it from what you say that the airplanes were bad for us?" Arnold Whiskeyjack asked in a voice louder on its own than Clarence's was on the speaker.

Clarence instantly fumbled: "I only meant to say—"

"We know what you will say even before it comes out of your mouth, Mr. Brody. We've been hearing it all our lives."

There were murmurs of approval around the gym. Clarence's pounding, burning ears could pick up Cree being spoken as Arnold Whiskeyjack's comments were interpreted.

"I only use the planes as an example of southern culture—"

Arnold Whiskeyjack sneered at him. "You speak as if they are your planes. They're our's—and I assure you, mister, they mean more to my life than they do to your's. Do you have any idea of what the level of infant mortality is here in the North?"

"Of course, I've read—"

"Read—good for you. Did you see the number for my mother's family? Did they have numbers for her two brothers and three sisters who are in the graveyard? Did you ever wonder why all my brothers and sisters are still alive? Does a book tell you that?"

"Look, I only meant that the planes bring in—"

"And take out. Don't forget that. They brought you in. They can take you out again when you're finished doing your 'good work.' A plane took me out when my appendix ruptured. And brought me back here alive."

Clarence felt a wave wash over him. He felt like he was being lectured by the Clarence of the movie he hated.

"That's the problem with your 'Preservation' Club, you know. You either want to lock everything in or go backwards."

"That's not true. I—"

"We want to keep lots of things, too. But what you don't understand is we want to keep lots of things we just got, as well. And we still want to get a lot of things. Like a doctor for the village."

"Of course."

"How do we get one, then? We pay him. Do you think there's still a doctor in Canada who'll work for the odd beaver pelt. How far back do you think we should go, anyway? Back to when the Hudson's Bay Company put a stupid hat on the most agreeable trapper's head and declared him chief? Back to when the Europeans took all the beaver, and half our people died in two winters?"

"Of course not. I've never said anything even remotely like that."

"You don't have to. You see us being destroyed now by something that is hurting us, but may also be helping us. And you see us being saved by going back when going back isn't possible—not even in your dreams, mister."

"I—"

"Don't feel sorry for us, Okay?"

Clarence had no time to answer. To a rising cheer and applause, Arnold Whiskeyjack turned and stomped out of the gymnasium. When Clarence looked back out on his audience, they were pulling on coats and talking so loudly he didn't dare try again. Chief Lucy Stringer gave him a lame smile and a shrug as she took away the microphone. The night was over.

"Merry Christmas," she said.

~~~

Clarence went home after the botched presentation and sat over tea with Beulah and Lanny, who had come back in from the bush for the pageant. He tried to explain how he had been misunderstood, and while they were sympathetic, they weren't much interested. Lanny wanted to recount the nativity scene. One of the grade-8 'wise men' had announced, in Cree, that the principal had just passed wind and would, in a moment, be coming up on stage to blame it on someone else. Sure enough, a moment later the red-faced, English-and-French-only principal had stormed up the steps with his fingers snapping and pointing. Every time he pointed at someone new, the place had broken up. Clarence laughed, but only out of politeness. He knew it could just as easily have happened to him. The whites were like a permanent cartoon for the villagers. The priest, the principal, the guy with the tape recorder.

The telephone rang and Beulah answered. It was a call for Lanny. One of the trucks headed further out the dump road had skidded off into the ditch, and they needed Lanny's four-by-four with the winch to haul them out. There was no asking, just need, and Lanny seemed delighted to go. He asked Clarence along for the adventure.

The four-by-four warmed up as they headed out, the front window eventually opening more than the small periscope circle Lanny had scraped for his own vision. For the first part of the ride, Clarence could only hear, and the sound he picked up was of Lanny's chains. The chains sang on the road, a sweet, comforting sound that took Clarence back to his own childhood before chains were outlawed because they tore up the new highways.

With nothing to look at, his own Christmases past came back to him. The chains reminded him of the difficult ride to his grandparents place in the country, and he remembered the Santa on the kitchen wall that would say "Merry Christmas" if you held your thumbnail hard to the back of a plastic string running out of Santa's mouth and pulled down hard. Clarence wondered whatever had happened to the plastic Santa. He looked down at his hands and wondered whatever had happened to his nails.

The windshield cleared by the time they reached the stranded travellers. No one was hurt. No one even seemed concerned. They had faith in Lanny's winch and the
~~~

tire chains. But the ditched truck was stubborn and would not give. Lanny ran the winch until he was afraid the cable might snap and the chains dug in but could not hold. The children in the truck were getting cold and one was starting to cry. Clarence gave up his seat in the four-by-four so the child could get warm again.

"Try putting something under the wheels," Clarence suggested when he got out.

One of the men seemed baffled. "What?"

"My father used to carry a rug around in case he got stuck. Something to grip."

"I got no rugs," Lanny called from the driver's window.

"What about branches?"

The men looked at each other and figured they may as well try Clarence's suggestion as any. Clarence found himself supervising, the master of new technology, and he directed the men to pile dry black-spruce boughs under each of the four wheels of Lanny's vehicle and then had a man stand at each corner prepared to feed in new branches as needed.

Some of the branches caught immediately and were spewed out the other side. Others were fed in, some caught, others caught, and suddenly the wheels caught and the winch yanked and the truck in the ditch jumped.

Clarence and two of the men went down into the ditch and Clarence got in under the bumper. "When I say 'Go!'" he found himself shouting up to Lanny, who nodded.

"Go!"

The four-by-four lurched but held. The ditched truck jumped, slipped, gunned its engine, jumped again and began moving, the men on the bumper pushing and falling and sprawling as it came out of the ditch as alive as a trout out of an ice hole. It was up, and free. The stranded family cheered and shook the hands of Clarence and Lanny until they finally had to just break away and go. Lanny's four-by-four—purchased on the guaranteed-income system of traditional hunting, tax deductible and amortized—was a resounding success. And so, too, it seemed, was Clarence. For once.

On the way back, Clarence found himself telling Lanny about his father's chains. He talked, and Lanny talked, and Clarence got to thinking about what had just happened and what Arnold Whiskeyjack had said to him in front of the entire village. The winter tire chains had seemed traditional to Clarence; but the chains went one direction for Clarence, the opposite direction for Lanny, for here they were new and obviously functional. Southern culture, imported, and paying off.

"You know," said Lanny, when they arrived back at the house, "you should really talk to my mother about Christmas. She has some great stories."

"I've tried to talk before. She won't."

"I'll get her to."

In the morning, Lanny made good on his promise. They lingered over breakfast and Lanny teased his mother until Ruth, smiling to herself, began to talk in a quiet voice. Lanny and Beulah took turns interpreting, and soon the rhythm became hypnotic, Ruth speaking slowly, sometimes laughing, Lanny and Beulah always laughing, the story repeated in English, and Clarence making a good show of laughing, which pleased Ruth and encouraged her to tell more.

As the morning went on, Ruth's voice took on that musical quality that the older Cree acquire when they are telling a long, involved story. It rose, danced, lingered, paused and rolled.

"She says the priests made a big deal out of Christmas but that she and her husband were always in the bush at Christmas. She says I was born around Christmas, maybe even Christmas Day, but she says it was too cloudy to see if there was a star overhead." Lanny and Beulah laughed loudly at this, and Ruth giggled again, sensing where her son was in the story.

"She says she used to hang socks in the lodge for us, and we'd go to sleep crying because Santa would never find us away out in the bush, but she'd fill up those socks with little things she'd gathered—maybe a pretty stone or some raisins or sometimes even a little toy. Something for every kid. She says it was the best time of their lives."

Clarence desperately wanted Ruth on tape but he could not stop the flow and set up. Hearing her talk like this was making him anxious, almost as if it did not exist if it had not been collected and catalogued. And yet, here she was giving him exactly what he was looking for in his reports. Something precious lost. Something beautiful and simple gone forever. If only her voice was not sounding into thin air, but into his recorder.

Ruth spoke for a long time, long enough for Beulah to brew another pot of coffee. Finally, the old woman finished, and Lanny was quiet for some time, considering how such a tale might be told in English.

"She told me a story I never heard before," he said to Clarence. "I only spent the first four winters in the bush, so I don't remember any of this. But she says we were so poor one winter—there was no beaver—that she had nothing at all to give us for Christmas. We were all crying and she didn't know what to. Our father was trailing caribou and wouldn't be back for days.

"My mother says she woke us up early Christmas morning and made us look outside. It had snowed during the night and was bright, bright, bright. You could hardly look. The snow was blowing a little bit and every time it lifted it seemed it had turned to gold the way it was sparkling in the sun, eh?"

Clarence nodded, unsure of the point.

"She told me and my brother and sisters that Santa Claus had come and turned the snow to white sugar. We loved white sugar because my father used to put it in his tea and we'd eat full spoonfuls of it. But he had none this winter. We couldn't even remember what it tasted like. She took a spoon outside and dipped it down onto the new snow and came back to where we were all looking out and told me I had to eat it real quick. She held it out, and I swallowed, and she says my eyes got real big, and I told the rest of them it was frozen sugar. She went and got a spoonful for each of them then, one at a time, and we all believed her. But then she said it was magic and would only work once, that it wouldn't taste like sugar any more. We wouldn't believe her and went out and started eating the snow with our bare hands, but it was just snow . . . "

For a long time Lanny sat, staring at his mother, shaking his head in delight. "We honestly believed Santa had been there and turned the snow to sugar. And she never told us any different."

Clarence looked at Ruth and nodded. The old woman was staring back—eye contact for once—and when Clarence looked he saw that her eyes were glistening. She sat in a room with a colour television, a VCR, stereo and, behind her, a kitchen with a microwave, dishwasher, electric stove, refrigerator and a pantry filled with sweets. And yet it was obvious she would trade it all for one more spoonful of that snow.

"Would your mother tell me that story on tape?" Clarence asked.

Lanny interpreted. He and his mother talked a long time, the exchange going back and forth like a tennis volley. Sometimes Lanny laughed, sometimes his mother, but she ended with her head slightly shaking, no.

"She says the story was for you, not a machine."

~~~

On the night of the feast, Clarence tried to watch television. He flicked through the satellite guide and found *It's a Wonderful Life* was on in four different time slots, but he would pass. He needed no further lectures from guardian angels or Arnold Whiskeyjack. Restless, he decided to write down at least a reasonable recapitulation of Ruth's story of the spoon and the snow. It was such a perfect rendition of simplicity lost that he knew it must not be lost itself.

He had just opened up the traditional file on his laptop when the first sound of singing found its way into the room. At first he thought Beulah must have left the kitchen radio on when the other three went out, presumably to the feast, but when it turned out not to be the radio, he went to the front door and ran the side of his hand over the frost to clear a view. There was a crowd outside, and the sweet, angelic sounds of "Silent Night" came faintly in through the weatherstripping. Clarence wondered why they had stopped here at this house. Possibly it was the stranded travellers and their friends come to thank Lanny for hauling them out with his winch. He would have to let them know no one was home.

He opened the door and stuck out his head. He felt the cold but also the sound, the voices crystal in the still night. Inside, he had been able to pick up the tune, but now he could hear the words. They were singing in Cree. And though it had sounded like the voices of children from inside, outside he could see that the choir was children and adults and even the very old. Ruth was there. And Beulah and Lanny.

They stopped singing. Lanny stepped forward.

"Get your coat and boots on, Clarence. You're playing."

Clarence had no idea what he was talking about. Playing what? An instrument? Clarence could not even sing. What did Lanny mean?

"Hurry up!" someone else yelled. "Come on!"

"What do you mean?"

"The broom-ball game—you're representing our neighbourhood. You're playing. Come on. Hurry up."

Clarence stood, his mouth open, his teeth aching from the cold. He did not play broom ball. They were pulling his leg.
~~~

"Come on, Clarence," Beulah called.

"Come on," a man called. It was one of the men from the stranded truck.

Clarence felt he had no choice but to close the door and go and dress for the outside. Baffled, still half convinced they were setting him up for something, he pulled on his boots, parka, toque and heavy gloves. Ready, he stepped back out the door only to find the crowd gone, the sounds of another song, "Noël, Noël" coming from down the road as they gathered yet another player.

Clarence caught up to the crowd and pulled up alongside Lanny and Beulah.

"There you are," Lanny said.

"What's going on?" Clarence asked. He was worried that the tone in his voice made him sound miffed. In truth, he was excited.

"East side of the village against the west—the Cree Cold War!" he laughed.

"Traditional Cree broom ball," someone else said, laughing.

Clarence turned abruptly. Beside him, grinning, with his hands in his pockets, was Arnold Whiskeyjack. Were they having him on?

"Why me?"

"Why me?" laughed Lanny. "I got a bad leg."

"I played last year," Beulah said. "We thought maybe you'd like a go at it."

Clarence hadn't even known about it last year. But then, he hadn't been here over Christmas. This was his first Christmas in the village, his first Christmas alone, he thought, now his first broomball game.

"But I don't even know how to play," he protested.

"That's fine—neither does anyone else.—

~~~

Someone had flooded the rink. And there were more lights than usual strung along the four telephone poles surrounding the open-air rink. The ice surface glistened, the boards, painted new this year, shone. People were already gathering tight to the tops of the boards, already shouting for their side, their breath exclamation points for each remark hurled.

Clarence could understand none of the shouting, but he still found himself swept up with the east-side team. He seemed, for the moment anyway, more accepted
~~~

than ever before. The majority of the players were women and Beulah was handing around Montreal Canadiens hockey sweaters for the east-side team to pull on over their ski jackets and parkas. The moment he pulled on the sweater, Clarence felt better than he had ever before felt in the village.

There were brooms in the shed for those who had not brought along their own. They were cut off short and taped for grip, and felt about as natural in Clarence's hand as a chainsaw, which he had also never before used. He had no idea what to do with it.

They were spilling out onto the ice from the bench, and Clarence followed suit, his boots slipping instantly up and in front of him, his back slamming onto the ice and his head following, the heavy toque saving his head from cracking like an egg. When the thump of the ice cleared he could hear them laughing. Lanny came running out with a hockey helmet.

"You Okay?"

"I guess. The toque protected me."

"You got the wrong boots for this game. Here—put this on right over the toque."

Without waiting for an answer, Lanny fitted the hockey helmet over Clarence's head. His head was still ringing. What about his boots? They were winter boots. They told him in Toronto good to 50 below.

But no good for broom ball. The other players—Clarence noted—all had special boots on that gave them grip and allowed them to run and then slide. He could only slide, and sliding prevented him from running, so he could essentially go nowhere fast and only creep along as if he were surrounded by the black dogs and too afraid of falling to take a step. When the ball came in his direction and he swung at it, the boots gave again and he went down hard on the helmet, the sound like a rifle in the cold night. Around the boards, they howled with laughter.

Clarence wondered if perhaps he had been suckered into this game. They had brought him along for comic relief. Every time he fell, they laughed and cheered. Every time he swung at the ball and either missed and fell or struck it badly and fell, they roared again. But who would set him up. Not Lanny? Beulah? What about Arnold Whiskeyjack?

Clarence tried to head up the ice toward the west end's net. He got some grip and ran a bit, sliding unsteadily, and they laughed and cheered as he rode the ice like a tightrope walker. The ball squirted out of a corner scrum, and instead of hitting at it, he stopped it first and then tapped it ahead, the way he had seen the others do it. It worked.

He was admiring his play when Chief Lucy Stringer and Mabel Shaapumin caught him in a sandwich. Lucy hit his feet out, and Mabel—as big as any player on the ice—hammered him into the boards. The crowd went crazy. Clarence's shoulder hit the boards, then his hip, then he heard the familiar crack of his helmet on the ice, another rifle salute to cheer the fans. He lay there on his back wondering if he was broken.

"You Okay?"

Clarence opened his eyes and looked straight up: his team-mate, Arnold Whiskeyjack. Had he come to gloat?

"Thanks very much," Clarence said with as much sarcasm as he could muster.

"Get in the game," Arnold shouted down at him. "Everyone's watching *you*."

Clarence cursed under his breath. Obviously they were watching him. That was why they had come, wasn't it? That was why they had stopped and picked him up along the way when he would have been far happier sticking at home with his room, his tape recorder and his reports. They were letting him know exactly what they thought about him. And it was just as Clarence had always expected: they held him in utter contempt. The anti-fur protesters were right—these were a cruel people. He wouldn't give them the satisfaction.

Clarence headed back up the ice, still slipping badly. Before he could begin moving, however, Lucy Stringer lost the ball trying to go around one of the younger girls from the high school. She hit the ball to Arnold Whiskeyjack, and Arnold neatly stepped around Mabel Shaapumin and slapped the ball hard up the ice toward Clarence, giving Clarence a three-line breakaway. He was able to turn just as Lucy and Mabel and several of their team-mates began digging in to give chase.

He stopped the ball and tapped it in front, then began running helplessly like the Roadrunner before he suddenly shoots out of the cartoon frame. But Clarence could not shoot anywhere. He seemed not even to be moving. Then, barely, one sole caught briefly, then the other, and he found some snow that had built up, he slid a bit, and suddenly he found himself moving in on the west end's goal. Clarence slipped and the goalie read it as a fake and went for it, opening up the side of the net. Clarence shot as he went down—and scored!

The hours after the goal blurred. Not because Clarence was knocked unconscious—though Lanny swore he had been—and not because he was drinking for there was nothing but tea and coffee at the feast. Time blurred because Clarence could not believe what was happening to him. He had, first of all, been invited to the feast. Well, perhaps not invited; he merely drifted over to the community centre with the broom-ball crowd, and no one ever said anything one way or another. He was inside and the feast was on, and Clarence was delighted to be there.

So much had happened, he could not process it. He had eaten beaver and moose nostril. He had been told stories the likes of which he had never imagined, and there had been promises to let him tape the stories if he thought they would do any good. He had spoken with Arnold Whiskeyjack who had explained to him, with a wide grin, why they had come to the house and invited him to play in the broom-ball game.

"Because we felt sorry for you."

Clarence wasn't exactly sure what Arnold Whiskeyjack meant by this, but he knew he would have to think about it—later, when the feast was done.

They ate and drank and told stories long past a time when any other non-alcoholic party would have broken up and gone home. But no one seemed to wear down, not the children, not the old ones. And there were still the presents to hand about.

Chief Lucy Stringer had dressed up as a Santa Claus, though no one for a moment seemed to think Santa was anyone other than Chief Lucy Stringer. The beard kept getting in her way as she read out the names and eventually she just ripped it off and handed it to a kid to wear. The gifts that had come up from Val-d'Or were handed around and opened, and Clarence knew beyond doubt, brought more pleasure to giver and onlooker than to receiver, who invariably seemed embarrassed by the generosity.

"Clarence Brody."

Clarence couldn't at first place where the voice was coming from, who was calling him. When he looked up, all were looking at him.

"Clarence Brody," Chief Lucy Stringer repeated.

He realized that Santa was calling him. Red faced, afraid this time his socks would slip, he made his way up to where Lucy was sitting and holding out a small wrapped package to him. He took it, smiling thanks, and retreated to the back of the room where he had no idea what to do with the gift.

"Open it," Lanny called over.

Clarence looked up. Lanny was sitting beside his mother, and Ruth was smiling at him, nodding agreement. He nodded back and began opening the tiny parcel.

Inside was a spoon. Not even a new spoon. A scratched and slightly bent spoon, much worn.

He looked back up, Ruth still staring at him. She said something to her son and Lanny nodded. He got up and came over.

"She says you should go outside now and see the snow."

Clarence looked over. Ruth was smiling in his direction, again nodding. He nodded back.

No one noticed when he took his parka from the back of the chair near the front doors. He pulled on his slippery boots, bundled up and headed out, the cold night air sharp on his face as he opened the door and closed it quietly.

Outside there was nothing. Nothing but silence, nothing but darkness. Clarence's eyes would not adjust, nor could his ears adapt. The events of the evening and now night still rang in his head.

He walked away from the building—alone, but for once no black dogs to stalk him—and as he walked his sight came back. The village was faintly glowing, the lights of the buildings washing along the snow. He walked up the hill and away from the light, and looked up. There were no northern lights, but the stars were so close it seemed he was standing in a jar filled with them, not under a sky so distant it felt flat. The night sky had such depth that Clarence felt he stood so high above the ground he had himself become part of the heavens. He could, if he wanted, become a true guardian angel. And he did want.

He kicked the snow and it flew, the surface so soft and fluffy that it must have fallen sometime between the end of the broom-ball game and the feast.

The spoon—of course, Ruth's spoon.

Clarence pulled it from his pocket and remembered his mother's admonition that he was never to stick his tongue to metal in cold weather. She knew a man who had a piece of his tongue missing because they had had to cut him off a school railing. Clarence shoved it back into his pocket to keep it warm.

But he had to try. He pulled the spoon free again and bent down low, running the spoon along the fresh snow that, if he flicked it just so and looked back toward the nearest light of the village, sparkled faintly like gold.

He dipped a full spoonful and held it up, smiling at the memory of Ruth's little joke on her children.

He opened his mouth, turned the spoon upside down on his tongue and his mouth exploded with a freshness so sweet it seemed he had never tasted anything like it before.

Shadows of Christmas Past

Christmas came early this year.

It arrived before anyone expected, dropping in on a cold evening when volunteer shoppers were gathering the courage to head out, one last time, into the money-sucking maw of the mall.

What happened was, the lights went out.

One moment, all was completely normal—television roaring, ghetto-blasters pounding, Christmas lights blinding—and the next moment, it was not normal at all.

It was totally black.

It was completely silent.

No one said a word. There was the sound of soft scrambling as the small bodies of children and kittens and dogs found their way to the kitchen, and then the quick scrape of match over sandpaper as a nearly forgotten light was produced.

Pale and yellow, it sent shadows leaping against the wall.

"Neat!" someone said.

The evolution of light was quick. From the bare match these deprived people soon moved on to a single flashlight and, with the flashlight, two ornamental coal-oil lights were located from another room and brought into the kitchen.

The children had never seen such magic.

"How do they work?" someone asked.

Good question. But, eventually, the hands remembered: the chimney carefully removed, the wick rustily twisted higher, a match dragged across its length and the wick quickly lowered.

Then, with the chimney refitted, the magic begins. With the wick brought up, the room is filled with a liquid yellow colour it has never before known.

The children stare at each other and their surroundings as if they have never seen them before; and certainly, in this light, in this quiet, they have not.

"It's beautiful," someone says.

The second lamp is lighted. There is something about the caution that surrounds the ritual of a coal-oil lamp that is, in itself, warming—almost as if, in taking light so much for granted, we have lost the awe.

"It's like being at a cottage," someone notices.

And everyone agrees. It is not just the light, but the silence, as if, for once, you might hear a squirrel scamper across the roof rather than the burst of a laugh track from the television room.

The littlest girl and the boy have taken the flashlight and gone to their bedroom and are back with comforters, which they wrap themselves in with exaggerated squirms of delight. They want a fire.

And while they settle, you go and stare out the window. Where there should be bragging Christmas lights, there is only discreet darkness now, the flickering shadow of neighbours moving in candlelight. The street lights are out. A car passes its headlights sweeping over the snow, and for once, you wonder what they are thinking rather than what they are driving.

The smaller children, wrapped like tomorrow's butterflies in their comforters, are filling in the space usually taken by television and cassette tapes. They are talking about camping and cottaging, trying to see who can recall the most treasured moment of the year just past.

"Remember the snapping turtle?" someone asks.

"Remember the deer tracks by the sandpit?" someone answers.

But I stand by the window remembering not deer tracks but another house in the bush when these same lamps would cast just enough light for an old ranger to work on his crossword puzzles and an old woman to prepare her Christmas baking.

The same silence, the same light, the same pleasure in small memories that would gather each Christmas.

"Remember the big toad?" a voice wonders.

But before anyone can, the power surges back on. Lights, television, tapes, buzzers, clocks...

"Boooooo!" the children shout.

It is a false surge. The power fails, the coal-oil lamps regain their place, the children cheer.

And while they are remembering more, we go about turning off every switch we can find, in the hope that they never, ever forget.

Angel with a Cowbell

Sip.

Puff. Puff-puff.

Puff-puff-sip.

Puff-puff-puff.

Sip . . .

. . . dot. Dash. Dot-dash. Dot-dot. Dash-dot. Dot . . .

". . . Trust this finds you well, dear Elaine."

Seven final words and Stanley Thornton was beat. Puffed out—and sipped out. Done. He had been writing since 7:00 a.m. Again unable to sleep. When the morning nurse came in to turn him over, he had asked to get up, and once up and washed and fed, he had asked the nurse to roll his computer over, and here it was, almost noon, and he had done nothing all the morning long but write, yet another time, to Elaine. Four hours at the keyboard, four hours sipping and puffing and resting. And yet, if he printed what he had written out, perhaps it would run three pages. Three pages. It wasn't as if he had been hard pressed for words. The words came to him easily. It was the vowels and consonants he had trouble with.

A puff for a dot, a sip for a dash. Five puffs for a 'p,' two puffs, two sips and two more puffs for a simple period. Communication amongu humans had gone from grunts and gestures to instantaneous transmission, and yet here was Stanley

Thornton trying to marry Morse code to a computer modem in order to get a message to someone he had never met nor spoken to. He was sitting at a machine that could transmit data at 14,400 chunks of information per minute, and yet he, Stanley Thornton, worked at approximately 32 letters a minute: dash-dot-dot . . . dot-dash . . . dash-dash . . . dash-dot. Damn. He sometimes thought he could sense his computer waiting on him, arms folded impatiently, one foot tapping in annoyance.

He was writing again to Elaine. It was, according to his file records, the 19th time he had written to her in less than seven months. Nearly three letters a month. This was on the verge of getting serious. He had no idea what she looked like. He knew her e-mail address, and he knew, from her letters back, that she lived in a small town outside Ottawa with her parents, her sister Charmaine, a dog and two cats. He knew that she was 33. He was 32. He knew that she had a job at the House of Commons (she didn't say what she did). He knew she worried about the country, had cried watching *The Remains of the Day*, secretly read the grocery-line tabloids, loved spring, and was crazy about the Montreal Canadiens.

He was a Leafs fan. Always had been. Always would be. He wore a Leafs sweater most days in winter, his old number—8—on the back with his name, Thornton, stitched above the number in striking white. He liked to kid her about the 1967 series when the Leafs had stunned the more-talented Habs; she liked to kid him that it was the last and would remain the last time the Leafs had won the Stanley Cup.

They had met by accident. He had been scanning the community discussion section on Freenet, and his eye had been caught by a simple notice thrown into the millions of bytes that pass through every day. "Help!" she had written. "Can anyone out there get me out of here?"

He had loved the idea: trapped on a bulletin board. Unable to go anywhere, unable to leave, the microchip as deserted island. He had sat all morning wondering if he should contact her. He could help. He had one of the best computer systems in town, certainly the best, by far, of all the outfits he had seen in the Algonquin Facility, where he had been living since the accident. The Dukes, his old team, had chipped in to set him up with everything he would ever need: computer, colour monitor, internal modem and fax, tube adapter for Morse-code control. Ted Larsen, his old centre man, who was now running the best computer store in Pembroke, had set it up and brought in an expert from the States to teach Stanley how to use the Morse-code system. Sip-puff-puff-puff. Puff-puff. Puff . . . puff-puff. Puff-puff. Sip-puff. Sip-sip-puff . . . B-O-R-I-N-G.

It had taken him two years to get to this point, but at least now he could work the machine, get into his files and access the various networks. He loved browsing: others had shopping malls, he figured, he had the bulletin boards and various networks to scour for interest. For a long while he had been part of an extensive hospital group that ran all the way from Fresno, California, to Saint John, New Brunswick, each member in rehabilitation, and every one of them anxious to find someone who understood.

Understood . . . It struck Stanley as a ridiculous notion. Why waste time searching for someone who understands when he could not understand himself? He had bailed out after a month of chit-chat, and signed off permanently. Not interested.

But Elaine's call for help interested him. Her question had seemed so sweet, so innocent, so helpless. He had written back—puffing and sipping into his tube, the words slowly forming, the codes quickly accessing—and he had made contact. His first communication was simply a note: he said who he was, how long he had been involved with Freenet and the Internet, how he would be glad to help. She wrote back saying she was having trouble working her way through the complicated menus, having trouble knowing where to go to get what she wanted—whatever that was. She called herself a Luddite and a Techno-nerd. He liked that. She needed him.

He stayed up half that next night working on a long letter. It amounted to a sort-of *Cole's Notes* to getting and staying on and getting off of the information highway. It was clear and concise; when you sip and puff every single letter, you learn to be concise. He sent it off to her. She wrote back to him with thanks, telling him a bit about herself.

And that's how it began. And this is how it appeared to be ending. He had started to tell her more and more about himself. He told her about his family and his home, about his brothers and sister and about the things he liked. He talked about books and movies and video games and celebrities and sports heroes and politicians. He talked about fishing and poison ivy and how he was afraid of electrical storms ("I'm not," she wrote back).

Through letter after letter he had proceeded to lay out his life story, always stopping just short. He had told her about the year he failed in elementary school, about the dogs he had owned, about the places he had travelled. He spent nearly three full letters talking about the sports he had played. He told her about the swim team and about the year he played lacrosse and the high-school volleyball team (City champions!) and all about the best ski hills in Eastern Ontario and Western Quebec.

But mostly he talked about hockey. His game. He told her about starting out in novice, and about the little goaltender who forgot to go to the bathroom before his father suited him up and who ended up flooding the ice before the game was half over. He told her about the year the rep coach came to watch the house league, and how the rep coach had come and talked to his regular coach and then to his father and then had come and asked him if he'd like to join the team for a tournament in Arnprior. He had, and he had never looked back. Leading scorer in pee wee. The Quebec Pee Wee Tournament. All-star in bantam. Midget, juvenile, a couple of years in Junior C.

And he told her all about his championship jacket. The colours—teal green and black—and the raised crests, and how the crest over the heart said Regional Champs, Senior Hockey. He did not tell her that he had never worn it.

He told her about the final series against the team from Renfrew, and how it had gone back and forth—the home-town team winning, then losing on the road—until it had all come down to that final game for the championship. He had scored in the first period, a lucky goal that had really been a pass that happened to scoot into the net off a defenceman's skate. The other team had scored. Then his team got two, the opposition got two and then—midway through the third period—he had the breakaway that ended up deciding the championship.

He told her he had been named Most Valuable Player of the play-offs. He told her that they had eventually retired his sweater, and that it was now on show behind glass in the front hallway of the community centre.

None of it had been a lie. He did not tell her how the breakaway ended, but it was a fact that this moment had decided the outcome. The last thing he remembered clearly was the sound of old Mrs. Humphrey's cowbell, the frantic clanging filling the rink as he shot ahead with the roar of the home-town crowd. The bell was ringing for him. He was old Mrs. Humphrey's favourite player. She even wore a button with his face on it—Stanley Thornton in full uniform, set to shoot, staring out with determination—and for two seasons now, she had announced when Stanley had possession of the puck with a loud, rhythmic clanging of the cowbell. The other teams despised it and often brought air horns to attempt to drown her out. But it never worked. When Mrs. Humphrey's bell sounded, it meant Stan The Man Thornton had the puck, and the enemy was under siege. It was the perfect musical accompaniment for his breakaway.

Mrs. Humphrey's bell was ringing when he went down. He had been tripped from behind, and when his feet went out, his head shot straight and uncushioned into the boards. When the game resumed—minutes later? hours later? days later? he wasn't sure—his team had been awarded a penalty shot which had resulted in a goal, which was the goal that decided the game. His penalty shot. His goal. The senior championship.

Only he hadn't taken the shot. His sweater had been retired because no one else would ever dare wear it, not after what had happened.

On the wall of his room in the Algonquin Facility was the team photo, taken moments after the championship trophy had been awarded. His team-mates—Ted Larsen front and centre—were surrounding it, some of them lying on the ice, some of them kneeling, some of them standing with their hands on the shoulders of those kneeling, young men, mostly in their 20s and some in their early 30s, all in the prime of life. It was a photograph that is taken a thousand times a year in this country, from the novice house-league championship to the Stanley Cup. Only this photograph was unlike all others. In this photograph, no one is smiling.

Stanley could not tell Elaine that he would soon count a full decade of his life spent in a wheelchair. He could not tell her that he had no movement from his neck down. He could not tell her that his letters took all day, every day, not that they were dashed off when he had time from his busy schedule. Dashed off . . . such a strange phrase for him. He could not tell her that he preferred to sign his letters "Stan" rather than "Stanley" because it took five fewer puffs and one less sip. Dash. Dot. Dot-dot

. . . dot-dot.

~~~

Ted Larsen felt like a sneak. It was none of his business and he knew it, but he couldn't help himself. Every couple of weeks, just as he had ever since the accident, he dropped in to the Facility to spend some time with his old winger. Usually it was just to drop off a rented video or a hockey magazine or a new computer game, but sometimes it was to fiddle with Stanley's set-up. Because of his business, Ted had become the local computer expert to family and friends and now, thanks to a lifelong
~~~

friendship with Stanley Thornton, to the entire computer operation at the Algonquin Facility.

Three months earlier, Stanley Thornton's hard drive had started to go wonky. Ted had taken the computer off for a few days and returned it in perfect condition, but to work on the hard drive he had first bled the files off onto several disks for safe keeping, made the adjustments, and then put all the files back. It was a simple procedure, routine, but in doing so Ted Larsen had ended up with all of Stanley Thornton's files copied to disks, which now lay on the desk in front of him. Normally he would have erased the files on the disks—but this time he hadn't.

Why had he snooped? He didn't know. He thought, at first, that he was simply checking on his old friend to find out how he was doing, and in some way, that was true. Stanley Thornton's progress had been extraordinary, and if anything spoke to that miracle, it was the material gathered on these disks. Stanley was taking college courses with the cooperation of the local school's outreach program. A couple of students had volunteered to record lectures and transcribe notes to disk and bring the disks to Stanley. He was six courses into a social-work program, all done by correspondence. It might take him five years more, but he would eventually be a graduate.

If that wasn't a miracle, Ted asked, what was? Ted had been on the ice when it happened. He had, in fact, passed the puck ahead to Stan. He sometimes wondered if perhaps he himself was partly responsible, for he could have bumped the defenceman cutting across toward Stan, and it was this player who took Stan's feet out from under him. It would have held some risk—Ted could have been called for interference, meaning the breakaway would have been whistled down—but referees rarely call interference late in the third periods of important games. Now, comparing the risk of a penalty to what happened, there was no doubt in Ted Larsen's mind as to what he should have done.

Just consider what had happened. When Stanley Thornton piled head first into the boards, his neck had snapped at the fourth cervical vertebrae. He had gone into convulsion. They had been so worried that they had brought the ambulance in through the Zamboni chute, loaded him on straight from the ice, and the ambulance had flown, lights flashing, back out the chute and straight to the Pembroke hospital.

Consider: a young man, then 23 years of age, in the prime of life, racing down the ice on skates one moment, racing off the ice in an ambulance the next. A young man who could, as they said, dance with the puck one minute, unable to move anything but his head and left shoulder the next. He went from a helmet to a halo, and from the halo to the wheelchair that he could operate by flexing his one working shoulder against a special pad fitted with sensors. It was, they said, a miracle that he was able to recover so much.

But why had Ted Larsen not been able to let it go at that? What compelled him to invade the privacy of his friend? He didn't know. All he knew was that he had started to scan through the files of Stanley's computer—cleaning up, he told himself at first—and had become more and more intrigued by this new life Stanley Thornton had created for himself through the Internet.

Ted not only had all the early letters that Stan had sent to Elaine, he had returned twice to "fiddle" with the computer—"I just want to see if maybe this communications program might be better suited to your modem"—and had deliberately, sneakily bled off the latest letters while he had been there. He now knew all about the stories Stan had been telling. And not telling. He knew about the lie concerning the hockey game.

Why had he done this? As a computer salesman and system installer, privacy was supposed to be a concern of Ted's. He knew all about passwords and security networks and viruses. But now he himself had become a lurker in his friend's system. A trespasser. Why?

He knew why. He felt responsible. Responsible for what had happened. Responsible for what happened after. He read on because he wanted to know how Stan would present the final game to someone who had not been there. He wondered at first if he would be blamed—"Of course, I would never have ended up in a wheelchair if my good friend, Ted Larsen, had done his job properly"—but his name hadn't even come up in any of the letters.

What had come up had been, in its own way, even more disturbing. Stan was lying to this wonderful woman who seemed more than willing to accept him for whoever he was—however he was. He had chosen a fantasy that did not involve the trip. He had scored the goal. He had seen his sweater retired. He was the local hero.

Ted felt an overwhelming urge to protect his team-mate.

Now, nearly a decade after he felt he had first failed him.

~~~
~~~

"Mr. Stanley Thornton,

mb238cFreenet.Carleton.CA

"My Dear Stan,

"Thank you for the wonderful letter of the 14th. I'm getting so I look forward to your letters more than anything else in the week. I like the idea of you writing every Wednesday and me answering every Sunday from now on, and I'll look forward to your Wednesday letter. I'll log on sometime around 7:00 p.m.

"Did you happen to see the movie, *Sleepless In Seattle*? I loved it. We're kind of like Sleepless in Pembroke and Sleepless in Ottawa. I love the way they talk to each other on the radio. It's kind of like us on the network. We don't even know what each other looks like!

"All I know about you is your age and that you have blond hair that you say is beginning to thin. But I don't know whether that means you look like Kevin Costner or Mr. Clean! Perhaps you should send a photograph so I can decide for myself.

"You never said whether or not you are still playing hockey. I imagine with all your courses and everything there's very little time for play, but a lot of people I know are playing late at night and I wondered if you were one of those—you know, "Every Thursday night, Stan and the boys get together for a little hockey and a few cold ones . . . " Are you still playing? I'd love to go to one of your games . . . "

~~~

Stanley Thornton had been staring at his computer screen for almost an hour. How could he tell Elaine the truth? He had conned her. He had lied to her. And now she wanted proof—she wanted to see him. Perhaps even see him play hockey. How would he ever get out of this?

~~~

Ted Larsen had an idea. He had been unable to sleep. He got up around 3:30 a.m., had gone downstairs, had made himself a big mug of hot chocolate, and he had sat staring at the back of a cereal box for nearly an hour when it came to him.

Why not let Stan live out his fantasy? It was his goal, after all, so why not let him enjoy it now, when he can. Look at how far he had already come. He was mobile. He was in college. He even had a girlfriend. So to speak. Electronically going steady, anyway.

Ted's first call had been to Rodney Chipperfield. He may as well begin with the most difficult one of all. If it fell apart there, there was little reason to go on. Rodney Chipperfield had been the player who had tripped Stanley Thornton. Now he was living in town and playing Sundays and Wednesdays with Ted's team in the "Gentlemen's League."

Ted knew how Rodney felt. Twice they had talked about it over beers after games. If Ted Larsen wished he had taken out the defenceman on that breakaway, the defenceman, Rodney Chipperfield, wished so much more passionately. If only Ted had taken Rodney's feet out from under him instead. If only it had been him crashing safely into his goaltender's pads, the puck already in the net, instead of Stanley Thornton going head first into the boards.

A fraction of a second. That is what had decided it for them all. Rodney Chipperfield had quit hockey for a long time after that game. He could not put up with the jeering and the insults. They called him "Crippler." He could only play now, he told Ted, because now there was never anyone in the stands. And anyone on the ice knew: they had all had their own moments when something goes wrong so quickly, almost always without consequence. But they all knew how easily it could happen.

"You know what they call that play?" Rodney had said the first time they talked about it.

Ted wasn't following. "What play?"

"The trip—when I hauled down Stan Thornton."

"What do you mean?"

"A good penalty—that's what they call it. You hear it every Saturday on *Hockey Night In Canada*. I hear it every game I ever watch. A good penalty. What a hell of a thing to say."

They met at the car dealership where Rodney Chipperfield was in charge of leasing. He heard Ted out and thought the idea ridiculous.

"You want to finish that game?"

"Yes. For Stan Thornton. He needs to finish it."

"He's in a wheelchair."

"There's wheelchair sports."

"Not for hockey."

But Ted wouldn't stop. He had thought everything out: chains, even, for the tires, a contraption that would flick a puck ahead of the chair and could be controlled by Stan, a proper ceremony for the retirement of Stan's sweater. One that, this time, he could attend. A new team photograph.

"He wouldn't come," Rodney said.

"He'd come."

"Who'd rig up the wheelchair?"

"Paul Farley and Derek Houser run a machine shop. They were on the team. They could do it. It wouldn't have to be that complicated."

"And why me?"

"You have to be there. You were there when it happened."

"I caused it to happen—remember?"

"It was an accident."

"It still happened."

"Besides," Ted said. "This time it will be different."

"How?"

"I intend to take you out this time."

~~~

Stanley Thornton woke up to the fire alarm thinking it was old Mrs. Humphrey's cowbell: clang-clang-clang-clang-clang . . . He had burst from a sound sleep and, when he realized what it was, thought it must be the Christmas tree in the common room. But almost instantly there was an announcement—False alarm—and he had been unable to get back to sleep, the bell taking him back again to that last rush up the ice, that final drive toward the net.

He had never for a moment felt any bitterness toward the player who had dumped him. He would have done it himself had the tables been turned, had done it himself, in fact, many times. Taken a 'good' penalty. Stupid thing to say, he thought.

A couple of times Rodney Chipperfield had come and visited Stan. He had never come alone—always with a team-mate or a mutual friend, once with Ted Larsen—and the visits had never been very comfortable, but they had been important to both of them and both of them recognized that fact. They never talked about the
~~~

trip---what could anyone say?---but in talking about everything else, Stanley's progress, Rodney's job, they had talked about nothing else, for the trip had become the point of departure for all that had since happened to both of them.

Stan figured he was up and may as well write Elaine. The faster he got with his Morse code, the more he seemed to be writing her. This was the second letter in less than a week. This was getting serious. With his shoulder, he pressed the alarm for the nurse.

Elaine had suggested they try using the chat system. They could log on and then sort of talk back and forth, one asking a question, the other answering, almost like a telephone conversation conducted on a keyboard. He hadn't answered her on that point. She must have wondered. After all, they had met because he had presented himself as a bit of an expert with the Internet. If anyone should be suggesting they move on to another level, it should be him, surely. He wondered what she had thought about him not answering her question. Did she think he had just forgotten? Or did she suspect he was hiding something from her?

Stan felt he couldn't. He wasn't fast enough. He would be staring at the screen if they did what she wanted and her questions would be coming up about as fast as a person can type and his answer might take 15 minutes. Puff-puff-puff. Puff . . . puff. Puff . . . puff-puff. Puff . . . puff-puff. Puff-puff . . . puff-puff. Not a single sip in "S-O-R-R-Y." She would wonder what was wrong. And he would eventually have to tell her.

In a way, he liked living on the Internet. There was a certain beauty to it. A certain freedom. People could only see what he was thinking, and his brain was the last bit of prowess he had left in this body that chose to ignore everything he told it to do. She liked what she saw of him through the computer. Perhaps she'd run if she saw him through the doorway.

~~~

"Ms Elaine Boudrias,

pw431cFreenet.Carleton.CA

"My Dear Elaine,

"Thanks for such a fine letter on Sunday. I've read it over two or three times and am very impressed by many of the insights you have. One day we'll have to talk at length---without typing!
~~~

"You asked about my hockey career after the championship. Well, I'd like to say I went on to play for the Toronto Maple Leafs and won the Conn Smythe Trophy when I led the Leafs to a four-game play-off sweep of the Montreal Canadiens ("Na-na-na-na, na-na-na-na, hey-hey-hey, na-na . . .")—but the truth is I did not. Senior champions was about as far as any of us got.

"Truth is, I haven't played much since. Oh, once in a while one of the guys like Ted Larsen—he was my centre—will call up about some ice time down at the old rink, and . . ."

~~~

They met at the Don Cherry sports bar. The waitress put together a few tables near the back, turned off the televisions and brought a tray of draft beer and diet cola for everyone. When they all had a drink, Ted Larsen laid out his plan.

They would give their old team-mate, Stanley Thornton, the Christmas present of a lifetime. He told them about Stan's new love interest in Ottawa, and how he had met her through the computer the Dukes had all pitched in on. No one asked Ted how he knew, and he didn't tell them about the damaged hard drive and his discovery. What did it matter how he'd found out? The important point was that Stan was doing fine, and he had a new, significant friend.

Ted told them how he had rented the old rink for this Sunday night and he told them that Paul Farley and Derek Houser had been working on the stick for Stan's wheelchair, and that they figured it would work fine. He could shoot a puck. He could score his goal.

Terry Bartholomew, who rarely smiled, asked the question everyone was considering: "Why?"

"It's his dream," explained Ted. "It was his goal. It would have been his penalty shot if he could have taken it. All we're going to do is let him put it in the net."

"And that's going to make him walk?" Bartholomew asked.

"Of course it isn't. But it's going to show him that we all remember who won us the championship."

"We dedicated it to him," said one of the others.

"Sure we did—but he wasn't there. He has the picture up on his wall, but he isn't in it. We retired his sweater, but he wasn't there."
~~~

"Does he know about this?" Bartholomew asked. He no longer seemed so negative.

"No."

"Don't you think he should?"

"We want it all to be a surprise. We're going to have someone special in the audience for him. We think it's time they met."

~~~

Ted Larsen had no idea how he was going to talk Elaine into coming up to Pembroke for Stanley Thornton's big game. He figured he'd call and wing it, as he'd winged everything in life. He was 34, in good health, had a job—winging it had worked fine so far.

"Elaine Boudrias, please."

"I'm sorry?"

His first thought was that he had made a mistake. He had taken her address from one of the letters—she must have put it in hoping that Stan would send her a picture—and her father's name had been mentioned in another letter. He had taken the man's name and the address and simply gone through Information. And now he had a wrong number.

"I must have the wrong number," he said.

"You want Elaine?"

"Yes—Elaine Boudrias. Does she live there."

"Yes."

"Can I speak to her please?"

There was a pause. "Does she know *you*?"

What is this? Ted wondered. An over-protective mother? A snoopy sister?

"No. I'm calling for a friend—Stanley Thornton."

"You're Stanley Thornton?"

"No. No. I'm Ted Larsen. I'm a good friend of his. I just wanted to speak to Elaine for a moment about something we're planning for Stan."

"I see." Another pause. "Well, Mr. . ."
~~~

"Larsen."

"Larsen—there's something you must not know about Elaine."

~~~

When he heard, Ted thought he understood everything. Elaine was there but could not come to the telephone because she could not talk on it. Her job at the House of Commons was to do the sign language for the hearing impaired. If Stan had been attracted to Freenet and Internet because he would not be seen and judged, she had come to it so she could be heard without having to speak. She was probably as worried about actually meeting Stan as he was of meeting her. Her sister brought Elaine to the phone and acted as go-between in a most unusual conversation. Ted told them about Stan—they didn't seem surprised; they said they knew there was something about him he was keeping to himself—and he told them about the plan to finish off the championship game the right way. The sisters loved the idea. They were anxious to meet Stan and they agreed to come up to Pembroke on the afternoon bus just before the game. They would have no trouble with getting away. Both worked on Parliament Hill and both were off for the Christmas break anyway. They would need a motel room to stay over, and would return to Ottawa the next day.

Ted picked them up at the downtown depot. They were obviously sisters, both dark and lively, both with the same childlike, charming smile. If there was a striking difference it was only to do with sound. The sister, Charmaine, was a talker; but so, too, was Elaine. Elaine, however, spoke with her hands, and Charmaine translated, the two so close and used to dealing with each other that, to Ted, the translation seemed instantaneous, Elaine's hands moving while Charmaine's voice read, with all the inflection and enthusiasm and humour that Charmaine possessed when she spoke for herself. They were a delight.

"What time's the game?" Charmaine asked aloud for her sister.

"Seven-thirty."

"Where's Stanley?"

Ted realized that Elaine was nervous, and the nervousness was captured perfectly in her sister's voice. Nervous and excited.

"Right after I drop you off, I pick him up."

"Are we allowed to cheer?" Charmaine asked.
~~~

"Of course. But just wait until we get him on the ice and he has the puck, okay?"

Charmaine's question hit him again. How could "we" cheer? Charmaine perhaps. But what could Elaine do? Perhaps Charmaine could shout for both of them. That seemed to be the way they worked together.

He dropped the women off at the motel just up from the rink, where he had already booked them a room. He wanted them at the rink before Stan arrived. Stan would have to know about the game before it began. The audience would hold the surprise.

Ted had made arrangements to pick Stan up at the Facility. He had told him they were going down to Ottawa to take in a junior hockey game at the Civic Centre. He would need the two hours they wouldn't be using on the drive down to rig up the chair and—though he hoped it wouldn't be necessary—to convince Stan to give it a try.

Ted felt an old familiar flutter in his stomach. The feeling he always had before a big game. A feeling he had almost forgotten.

~~~

"No."

"Why not?"

"I have no intention of making a fool of myself."

"Then we'll all be making fools of ourselves together. Half the guys are going to be there. Rodney Chipperfield is coming."

Stanley Thornton couldn't follow. His head was spinning. "Why would he come?"

"Same reason you should come. Same reason I'm coming. We want you to see your face when your goal goes in."

Stanley shivered. He had always wondered what it would have felt like. He had the team photograph—him missing—none of them smiling. They looked like they had just lost the world, not won the championship.

"I never scored."

"It was your penalty shot."

"You took it."
~~~

"I took it for you. There was no way on earth that puck wasn't going in. I'm convinced even their goalie felt that way."

"It makes no sense."

"C'mon, Stan—why does everything have to make sense. We're bringing a photographer. We're going to take a new photo."

"What?"

"Yah—with you. MVP, Senior Championship."

Stanley did not know what to think.

"Would you want a picture with us all in it? Everybody smiling?"

"Maybe."

"Then let's go—what've you got to lose."

~~~

His dignity, for one thing. He could lose his dignity. And his mind. The way things were starting to spin on Stanley Thornton he did wonder if perhaps he was going crazy. This was nuts. But still, he let his mad friend get out the Facility van and he let him load him on and now they were headed down Main Street toward the rink. Stanley had been back dozens of times since the accident. But he'd never felt like this. His stomach was turning over. He had to laugh: not supposed to have any feeling below his shoulders, but he could feel a game coming on.

Everyone else was already there. Ted helped him wheel into the dressing room, and the sensation was overwhelming to Stan. He could smell their fetid equipment-perfume to long-time hockey players. He could hear, even before the door opened, the take-no-prisoners insults that are the great equalizer of a hockey dressing room. He could hear Lanny Dowbigging asking to borrow some shin-pad tape—still cheap, after all these years.

When the door opened, it did not open at all as Stan had imagined. He thought he would bring things to a halt.

He thought he would be invading, that they would stop, out of respect, and everyone would act sheepish and ask about him and centre him out and make him feel like he was some sort of imposition on them. But it didn't happen that way at all.
~~~

"You're 10 minutes late, Thornton!" a big voice said from behind the partition. It was Curly Simmons, their old coach. He looked around the corner and frowned at Stan. "You're fined one round of beer after the game." They cheered and threw towels at Stan. A couple of the guys moved over on the bench, and Ted wheeled him through the clutter and spun him around so he was sitting where he usually sat, between the goaltender, Sid Bartholomew, and the big defenceman, Serge Dumont. Dumont seemed slightly irritated that he had to move his equipment bag over. Just like always.

Paul and Derek came in with the electronic stick. It was remarkably simple: a stick blade attached to a metal plate, the plate hinged to another plate that fitted onto the front of his wheelchair, the hinge operated by a small electric device that was wired back up along the back of the chair and fitted to a pulse button they tucked in behind his shoulder.

"Shoot!" said Paul.

Stan leaned back hard on the little button. The stick swung quickly out, quickly back.

"Gunner!" someone shouted.

They were acting as if all this somehow made sense, when it so obviously didn't. But as Ted had said, what did it matter? It was Christmas.

~~~

They horsed around awhile on the ice before Stan got his shift. The Dukes played a little no-contact shinny against the Lumberjacks. Rodney Chipperfield was on the ice and only once did he acknowledge Stan's presence, and that was with a little nod and a slight smile as he passed by the exit where Stan sat waiting, behind the glass. They had opened up the glass display case in the hall and removed the retired No. 8 sweater and now Stan had it on. It even smelled the same as they had slipped it over his head. He had hockey gloves on. He had a helmet on. His tires had been wrapped with what looked like chicken wire. "Chains," Ted Larsen had called them, and chains they were.

When they got the score to 3-3, the score that they had reached in the third period of the championship, they came down and opened the big doors where the Zamboni usually came out and Ted Larsen helped start Stan out onto the ice. The
~~~

last time he had been through these doors he had been in an ambulance. He was certain he could feel his stomach churn.

He came out with every player on the ice tapping his stick in salute. The fallen hero arisen. He tried his controls and the wheels spun, caught slightly, and he moved out slowly, slightly drifting past the net, and the Lumberjacks goalie gave him a big swat on the rear of his chair as he passed him by. With Ted's help, he wheeled down to the other end. He tried to turn and look around as he moved down the ice, and he was sure he saw someone sitting in the stands, but he couldn't make out exactly who. They set up—a breakout pattern—in their own end, and one of the other players came and took hold of the chair's handles and began moving Stan down the ice as the Lumberjacks began skating backwards in defence.

Ted, of course, was carrying the puck, just as he had before the trip. He came out over the blue line, danced around one check, tucked the puck in between the legs of another player and burst over centre looking for Stan on his left. He passed, just as he had that night so many years ago, and the player helping Stan stopped the puck with his glove and set it onto the electric stick at the front of the chair. Small grooves on the blade kept the puck steady, and the player gave Stan one final push toward the opposition net and left him on his own.

He could hear the sounds of skates behind him. He didn't need to see to know what it was. It would be Rodney Chipperfield in full chase.

He could hear old Mrs. Humphrey's cowbell. Clang-clang-clang-clang. . . The same rhythm that had filled his ears that night just before . . . He couldn't believe the detail Ted and his team-mates had gone to. They had even brought out old Mrs. Humphrey.

He heard a collision behind him and then, out of the corner of his eye, he caught sight of Rodney Chipperfield spilling by, a fallen Ted Larsen following. Both of them were laughing.

There was now nothing between Stanley Thornton and the net. The goalie was rapping his pads and wiggling out fast to cut off the angle. Stan instinctively pressed back on his controls and sped up, the chair catching, drifting slightly, and moving across the plane of the net.

It happened entirely by instinct. He could not even see the puck or the stick, but he knew by his eyes that the net was directly in front of him. He pushed back hard on the button. He saw nothing for a moment, then the puck emerged from below his knees, scooting along the smooth ice toward the net, the goaltender doing the splits, the puck cut off from sight until, a moment later, a red light flashed behind the sprawling goaltender, surprise somehow registering on his mask.

And then it began. The cowbell, the cheering, the whooping, the sticks tossed, the hugging, the spinning of Stanley Thornton's chair, the ruffling of hair, the slapping, the yelling, the tears.

It was as if the emotion had been piled up for all those years and now, suddenly, it had been released. Stan Thornton was crying. He wanted to cry. Needed to cry.

They were all in tears, including Rodney Chipperfield who was lining up with his team-mates for the customary handshake. The two teams went down the line, each tapping each other, congratulating each other, no one acting as if Stanley Thornton was in anything but full uniform and accepting his due. Rodney Chipperfield gave him a special hug. The Lumberjack goaltender dropped the puck in his lap. His puck, his goal.

They lined up with the trophy for the team photo. Sticks sprawling out in front of them, helmets off, hair wet, all of them finally smiling. Stanley Thornton, MVP, winning goal scorer in the centre of it; Ted Larsen, who had set him up, beside him, his arm wrapped around Stan's head.

The cowbell sounded, a final salute.

"I thought old Mrs. Humphrey had died," Stan said to Ted.

"She did."

"Who brought the cowbell, then?"

"You'll find out in a minute."

The Magic Knife

You would expect that your very first memory would go back to something that happened in your home, or at least within your family. You know---a special birthday present, a new sister, a badly cut finger, the first lick of a puppy, a terrifying electrical storm.

But not for me. When I think back as far as I can, I end up in the house directly across the street, crouching in Freddie's living room. It is Christmas and we are beside the tree. Perhaps you can smell the spruce, sweet as the scent from the cardboard tree that dangles from the mirror of his father's Edsel. Maybe you can hear his mother following the play-by-number chart on the new Hammond organ, her clumsy fingers finding the keys so slowly they will have to rename the tune "Silent Week."

But none of that matters. Freddie is showing me his new present. My very first memory is of a knife, a heavy, shining red Swiss Army knife that has more secret blades than a haunted castle has hidden rooms. The knife is in Freddie's fat little left hand. His right hand is picking out the treasures, one by one: three blades, scissors, screwdriver, corkscrew, Allen key, nail setter, magnetized Phillips screwdriver, small chisel, knife, fork, spoon, leather punch, bottle opener, can opener, rat's tail file, flat file, rasp, toenail clipper and, discreetly slotted into a small hole on one end, a stainless steel toothpick.

And that covered only one side of the knife. Still, Freddie wanted to move on to the next present in a row that lacked only the "Eaton's Toyland" sign overhead and Punkinhead running about beneath with a fistful of candy canes to hand out. I innocently picked up the knife as he let it roll back into its box. That was a mistake. Freddie grabbed me by the throat, his nails digging in.

"Hands off!" he screamed.

"I wanna see the rest!" I gasped.

"It's not yours!"

Before I could twist free, I felt the hands of Freddie's father on my arms, his hands so much bigger than Freddie's but the nails digging in the same way. It hurt and I began to cry. Freddie's mother had left the keyboard and was helping him to his feet, lifting Freddie so gently you would think a car had struck him.

"That's enough of that, boys." Freddie's father said sharply to me. "Maybe you'd better go home now," Freddie's mother said to me. "You have your own Christmas."

~~~

That was all several years ago. We still have our own Christmas, and at the moment I am lying in my bed waiting for movement downstairs, the signal that will allow me to get up, race down and act surprised by the skates I tried on last Thursday at Canadian Tire.

The light is on, and I can see every Freddie I have ever known. The near wall has been covered in framed class pictures that go back to the first year we lived in this neighbourhood. It is a perfect record of the two of us growing up together.

Actually, I'm still waiting for that spurt everyone swears is just around the corner. The length of the class pictures, you will see Freddie ballooning from the front row to the very back, while I travel year by year from back row to front. What separates me most from picture to picture are my clothes. Big for grade 2, I am a runt in grade 7. Same old freckles, same old cowlick.

With Freddie, the only consistency is in his face: squinty, mean eyes, and that grin that always makes you feel like you'd better check your back for a taped on cardboard insult. In the last picture on the wall, he's standing just behind Patricia Potts, and if you look very carefully you can see the scissors of his wonderful knife nudging up to her right braid.
~~~

The knife is still as shiny and red as ever, and five years after I first grabbed for it under Freddie's Christmas tree I have yet to put a hand on it again . That certainly isn't meant to imply that I still have no idea what treasures are contained on the other side of it. Just listen while I explain.

Barely two weeks after we'd had our little fight over the knife, we had another. This time there were no parents around to break us up and send me packing. We were on a snow bank down toward Main Street, two broken snow angels hanging upside down and watching the cars go by. Freddie had swiped Patricia Potts' mittens from the cloakroom and was using the scissors to lop the thumbs off before dropping them at the lost'n'found. When he finished, he snapped the scissors back in and began stuffing the huge knife back into the same pocket that always held a ball of Kleenex and a wad of fluff-coated candy from his grandmother's treat bowl.

"Lemme see the rest," I said.

Freddie shook his head, no.

"Please . . . "

"It'll cost you."

I looked at him angrily. "I haven't got any money---you know that."

"I'm hungry."

"So go home."

"I want a nickle grab bag from Turley's."

"I haven't got a nickle!"

"So."

I looked at Freddie. He was smiling that smile, his pig eyes tight and waiting.

"What's that supposed to mean?" I asked.

"Go steal me one."

I breathed deeply. Stealing was becoming Freddie's big thing. He always had money, but he'd rather steal as if it somehow improved the taste. Whenever we went into Turley's smoke shop he would later pull a Milky Way or a Jos. Louis from his pocket, and though he'd been encouraging me to join in the fun, so far I'd resisted.

"No way."

"Then no knife."

"How many blades will you show me?" I asked, just to see.

"Two."

Two minutes later I was standing in Turley's. There were older kids hanging around the Bluebird jukebox arguing about whether Sheb Wooley would outlast Elvis Presley, and a couple of big kids over by the magazine rack, giggling at the clouded-out areas in one of the nudist magazines.

Mrs. Turley sat by the space heater at the back of the store, her bad leg stretched out on a stool and covered by a blanket, and she was right then creating more of her special grab bags. She was surrounded by boxes of jujubes, banana fluffs, black balls, sour gum, hot stuff, wax lips, licorice lace and candy cigarettes, and when she had filled each little brown bag she spun it once for closing and then tossed it the four feet or so to the large wicker basket that held the Scotch-taped sign: Grab Bags 5¢.

I stood in front of the pen rack pretending to be searching for a certain colour, but really waiting for a customer to come along and distract Mrs. Turley. A man came in asking for Daily Mail tobacco, and when she turned to look, and he leaned to help her, I dipped down quickly, scooped a bag and was out the door.

Freddie was sitting straight up on the snow bank when I got back. I checked back, just in case Mrs. Turley might be hobbling up the street after me, then handed over the treasure.

"Just one?" he said, taking the bag greedily.

"One's all you said."

"I didn't say one and I didn't say one million."

He opened the bag, poured out some of the contents into his palm, then hoisted the handful to his mouth for dumping. The remainder joined a week's worth of other gum and caramel and licorice in his pocket that would come out later during reading time in social studies.

"Okay," I said. "Let's have that look."

Freddie looked at me as if he'd forgotten.

"The knife," I said, holding out my hand.

"You don't touch it," Freddie said, chewing. "I show you."

"Okay."

He pulled out the knife, separated it from the handful of used Kleenex and saved toffee that came out with it, then held up the side not seen that Christmas morning. He pulled one of the catches.

Even today, just remembering that moment, I cannot believe it happened anywhere but in a dream.

When the blade had completely revealed itself, we were sitting beside an aluminum four-seater toboggan.

I could hardly speak.

"I don't understand!" I said.

"Nobody asked *you* to understand, jerk. You asked to look."

"But how did it get in there?"

"What's it to *you*?"

"You said *you'd* show me two."

"Never did."

"Did so."

Freddie turned back with his special smile. "Pull me home," he said, "and I'll show *you* another when we get there."

He had me trapped and he knew it. I had to see more of the knife, even if it meant getting in harness and dragging Freddie home over the salt and sand and bare patches on the road. Sweating, wheezing, dizzy and sore, I got him to his driveway, where I dropped the toboggan rope and fell backwards into the cool snow.

"Here!" Freddie shouted as he headed for his door.

I turned and he had the knife out and his hand was yanking on another blade and suddenly I was holding a brand-new pair of Tackaberry skates, the best money can buy.

In some ways, it was fortunate for me that Freddie was growing and I was not. I was able to pass off the new skates by telling my parents that Freddie had received them from an aunt for Christmas but they had been too small and she hadn't included the receipt.

After that, whenever Freddie would pull things out of that incredible knife—baseball cleats, a fishing pole, a B B gun—I was able to pass them off as hand-me-downs.

Not that my parents much seemed to expect explanations. It was almost as if, if it came from Freddie's house, it was all right with them.

But not growing had its disadvantages, as well. The bigger Freddie got the more he came to bully me, until it seemed as though the day I dragged him home on the knife's toboggan was nothing more than a typical day in a fairly miserable life.

I had become Freddie's slave.

We would go to the beach, and he would pull out the raft the knife held, and I would have to dive for clams for him to skip at the girls swimming out to it. He would show me the colour television it held, and I would do his homework for him in exchange for a chance to watch the set with him during recess. He would show me the grade-5 history exam the knife had on one of its arms, but would let me see only half of the answers. If anyone was going to score perfect on the test—and one did—it was going to be Freddie. But since I came second in the class with 84 per cent, I could hardly complain. It was better to know part of the knife than to know nothing of its marvels.

Imagine my surprise, then, when this Christmas came around and Freddie had a gift for me.

Freddie surprised me by showing up at the back door first thing in the morning. It was freezing cold—his cheeks were white with frost. I could hardly believe it. Usually, in this kind of weather, I would be summoned to his house.

"C'mere," Freddie hissed.

"Wait'll I get dressed."

"C'mere!"

I went outside, my socks sticking like glue to the frozen snow. Freddie cocked his knife and shot out a blade. A German Shepherd puppy with a red bow around its neck wiggled off the end and immediately began plowing its nose through the snow. Freddie offered his special smile.

"His name is Duke," he said.

"Duke?"

"You heard me. He's *yours*."

"Mine?"

"You heard me."

"But why?"

" 'Cause I'm allergic, that's why. You keep him here. But he's still mine."

Duke ran over and jumped at me, his licks freezing instantly on my cheeks. He wiggled in the door and was gone, his tail hammering against the kitchen cupboards like a club.

I looked at Freddie. "Thanks."

"Just remember who really owns him," he said.

It was easy for me to remember, but not for Duke. My parents accepted the explanation immediately, as they always did whenever Freddie's knife was involved. Freddie had received the puppy for Christmas but his allergies had acted up and he'd decided to give the dog to me instead. How thoughtful of Freddie, they said.

By noon Duke was treating me as if we were part of the same litter. He lay his head in my lap as we ate Christmas dinner, slept on my feet as I watched *Miracle on 34th Street* in the afternoon, and bounded out the door ahead of me when I got the call from Freddie to bring him out where Freddie would be able to pet him but not be affected by Duke's hair.

Freddie was waiting by the street light, wrapped up so tightly only his eyes were squinting out. But that was all that was necessary to know something was in the works. Duke bounced over and jumped up on him nearly knocking Freddie over. Freddie swatted angrily at the puppy but missed as Duke darted off to investigate the artwork of other dogs along the far bank. Freddie had the knife in his hand.

"Call Duke over," he ordered.

"What for?"

"Just get him over here. You'll see."

I called Duke and he bounded over, first deking me as he came, then jumping for a lick. I grabbed onto his collar and held tight. The puppy pulled, then turned to watch Freddie, his eyes straining so I could see the whites and, I was sure, fear.

Freddie flicked the knife and a small dog sled and harness settled in the cone of light that spread out from the street light.

"Hitch him up!" Freddie ordered.

"He's too small," I argued.

"Hitch him up!"

Freddie reached out and grabbed the collar, *yanking* Duke toward the harness. The dog squealed. Freddie slapped hard across Duke's ear and the puppy went down onto his back, whimpering and lifting his rear leg.

"Help me!" Freddie shouted.

I began to hook up the dog. The harness was too large, but Freddie used the punch on his knife to make extra holes in the leather so it fit tightly around Duke's head and muzzle and over his shivering back.

Freddie stood back, satisfied.

He walked over and settled into the sled.

"Pull me down to Turley's!" he commanded.

"He can't!"

"The two of *you* can!"

I went to the front of the harness and pulled. Freddie was easily twice as heavy this Christmas as he had been that first time when I had pulled him myself in the opposite direction. The tension was on Duke's nose, and he whined as he pulled back, resisting. Freddie whipped him from behind and the little dog dug in, pulling just enough that the sled gave and began moving along slowly under our pull.

I worked as hard as I could, *yanking* and pulling and tugging and pleading with Duke to do what he could do. But it was no use. The dog was shaking badly and whimpering. I began to undo the harness.

"What do *you* think *you're* doing?" Freddie shouted from the sled.

"He can't do it!"

"So what? Make him!"

"You'll kill him!"

"So what? He's mine to do with as I please."

I released the puppy and he darted off, barking and tossing fresh snow with his nose.

Freddie got out of the sled.

"What did *you* do that for?"

"You can walk!" I said.

I was shaking. I had never challenged Freddie before.

"What did you say?"

I was scared. He was nearly twice my size, certainly twice my weight.

"You can walk," I tried in a reasonable voice. "It won't kill you. Besides, Turley's won't even be open."

Freddie hit me, a long windmill slap across the face that sent me spinning, and burned like snow on a frozen toe. I fell onto the road, scraping my cheek on the grit. Freddie began kicking me. I couldn't move. Duke came running, but this time not to jump and lick.

The puppy was growling, and he flew over me to land directly in the centre of Freddie's chest, pushing him back onto the sled.

Freddie screamed. As he turned he pulled the knife out of his pocket, and with a sudden snap, Duke simply vanished. I got up slowly, the fight gone.

"What'd you do with my dog?" I asked. I was crying.

"Your dog?" Freddie laughed as he got to his feet. "My dog—remember?"

"You gave him to me. He's mine."

"He's nobody's now, pal," Freddie snickered.

I don't know how it happened, but I hit Freddie then. Not so much a punch as a belly bump, and though I am so much smaller I must have caught him off guard, for back down he went.

He started to howl again.

He had the knife again in his hand. There was that same snapping sound. Then, nothing. Nothing at all but darkness. And the taste of metal. And the sweet, disgusting smell of the inside of Freddie's pocket.

~~~

Perhaps it is only appropriate: Freddie's house at Christmas, the first memory, and now the last memory, Freddie's house at Christmas.

Freddie's mother is listening to Billy Vaughn on her new stereo, his father is mixing a drink with too much ice. I can see nothing, but there is no problem hearing. My parents are on the next blade over, but whether they are giving me the silent treatment or are not able to speak I cannot say.
~~~

Duke is on a blade to the far side, his feet jiggling in a dream about running free. Freddie is already compiling his next year's Christmas list, telling his father what he expects.

"It'll depend on how good you are over the year," his father warns through an ice cube in his mouth. Freddie, of course, pays not the slightest attention.

"And I want a new knife, too," he says.

"Whatever on earth for?" his mother asks.

"I think I should have some new friends this year," Freddie says.

"Be a good boy," his father says, "and you'll get what you ask for."

The Day the Ice Turned to Glass

It was a case of nature answering the call.

It was the end of the worst year in the history of sports—a discouraging year when the main players wore suits instead of uniforms, and all available statistics began with a dollar sign—but finally, mercifully, it was closing down.

A new year, new hope.

It had snowed toward the end of the worst year, but the snow had melted and hardened in patches. Right up until the end, the water remained open.

But then, on the very last day, a deep, bitter freeze descended. It fell over the open water and, overnight, four inches of solid, clear glass formed on the creek on the far side of the road.

Glass ice: something that happens only every few years—and it is not to be missed.

"The Eskimos," Margaret Atwood once wrote, "had 52 names for snow because it was important to them."

That figure has been much debated since she used it, but hockey players may have even more names for ice: new ice, old ice, bad ice, spring ice, choppy, rutted, scab, crystal, soft, hard, open, lake, slough, pond, creek, backyard, school yard, artificial, free . . .

The best, however, is glass ice. It is rare, and comes itself in two varieties. The first is what the Scots called verglas and is a fluke caused by a snowfall followed by rain followed immediately by a deep freeze.

In *The Game of Our Lives*, Peter Gzowski once described the day he and his boyhood friends came across this miracle in Galt: "The snow held again, and off we went, soaring across roads and frozen lawns . . . forty of us, fifty of us, gliding across farmers' fields, inventing new rules for our unending game, allowing for fences in the middle of a rush, or goals that might be half a mile apart. I didn't know if that had anything to do with hockey . . . but I know I'd never been happier."

The second variety is the glass ice that follows a hard, unexpected freeze when there has been no snow.

Some people noticed it when out walking the dog. They came back and got sticks and skates and neighborhood kids and all set out for the walk out of the suburbs, across the road, past the farmhouse and down to the creek where the rare ice was waiting.

The kids had never seen anything like it. They lay on their stomachs and stared down where the water was still moving over the gravel. A minnow darted, frightened by unexpected shadows.

Had the minnow looked up, it would have seen Canada.

It would have seen children racing and sliding and laughing. It would have seen long searches through the bulrushes for raised pucks. It would have heard a country's forgotten rhythm, wooden sticks on a puck.

Here was Long Pond, Newfoundland, in the early 1800s, McGill in 1875, Queen's versus the Royal Military College in 1886. Here was the frozen pond, the river, the slough, the backyard. The Patricks and their wooden puck off Nuns Island, Maurice Richard on the Rivierès-des-Prairies, Walter Gretzky's backyard rink at 42 Varadi Ave., Brantford, Ont., Bryan Trottier out on the Saskatchewan, slough with Rowdy playing goal, not a tooth left in the old dog's head.

At one point, where the creek and the glass ice stretched straightest from one twisting corner to the next, we held a hockey game. No corporate boxes, no tickets, no lockout, no doom, no gloom.

We played for three hours until the kids could think of nothing to do but lie flat on the ice and stare down through the magic that may happen only once more in their childhoods.

"We shouldn't tell anyone," one of them said when we were walking home.

Oh yes we should.

People in this country need to know there is still a game out there, waiting.

For more copies of

Roy MacGregor's

Valley Christmas

send $14.95 plus $4.50 to cover
GST, shipping and handling to: